20th Century Linens and Lace

A Guide to Identification, Care, and Prices of Household Linens

Elizabeth Scofield
and Peggy Zalamea

Schiffer Publishing Ltd
77 Lower Valley Road, Atglen, PA 19310

Dedication

This book is dedicated to Ms. Elisabeth G. Speck
and Dr. Leonard Greene Scofield.

Printed in Hong Kong
ISBN: 0-88740-826-5

We are interested in hearing from authors
with book ideas on related topics.

Published by Schiffer Publishing Ltd.
77 Lower Valley Road
Atglen, PA 19310
Please write for a free catalog.
This book may be purchased from the publisher.
Please include $2.95 postage.
Try your bookstore first.

Library of Congress Cataloging-in-Publication Data

Scofield, Elizabeth.
    20th century linens and lace : a guide to identification, care, and prices
household linens / Elizabeth Scofield and Peggy Zalamea.
        p.   cm.
    Includes bibliographical references and index.
    ISBN 0-88740-826-5 (hc)
    1. Household linens--History--20th century--Collectibles. 2. Lace and
making--History--20th century--Collectibles.
3. Needlework--History--20th century--Collectibles. I. Zalamea, Peggy.
Title.
NK8910.S36 1995
746.9' 09' 04075--dc20   95-1190
                                                                        CIP

Contents

ACKNOWLEDGMENTS 4

INTRODUCTION 5

CHAPTER I   - APPENZELL AND APPENZELL-TYPE EMBROIDERY 7

CHAPTER II - BATTENBERG AND OTHER TAPE LACES 33

CHAPTER III - BOBBIN LACE 41

CHAPTER IV - CHEMICAL LACE AND OTHER MACHINE LACES 59

CHAPTER V   - COMBINATIONS OF LACE 71

CHAPTER VI - CROCHET 93

CHAPTER VII - CUTWORK 111

CHAPTER VIII- EMBROIDERY 121

      Eyelet Embroidery 121

      Whitework 121

      Multi-colored Embroidery 121

CHAPTER IX - FUN LINEN 133

CHAPTER X   - LINEN DAMASK 139

CHAPTER XI - NEEDLE LACE 145

CHAPTER XII - FILET LACE AND BURATTO 167

CHAPTER XIII- TATTING 177

CHAPTER XIV - TYPES OF DRAWNWORK 181

      Drawnwork 181

      Mosaic & Punchwork 181

CHAPTER XV - MAINTAINING THE COLLECTION 190

      Market Conditions 190

      The Art of Collecting 191

      Pricing 196

      Investment Potential 197

      How to Sell 198

      Care and Maintenance 198

BIBLIOGRAPHY 203

PRICE GUIDE 204

INDEX 206

Acknowledgments

We wish to thank the following people:

Ndidi Amachi

Kathy Biddle

Debra Bonito

Anna Burns

Trudy Clarkson

Roger Crockett

Joyce Taylor Dawson

James C. Ford

Tracylee Guerin

Monika Idler

Anne Warner Jean-Richard

Annie Kapetanis

Victor Lipkin

Rachel Maines

Robert McIntyre

Kay Mertens

Samantha Owen

Kathy Quarino

Robin Sabalones

Textilmuseum mit Textilbibliothek

Suthira Zalamea

Introduction

The linens and lace illustrated in this book represent the whole array of collectible household linen made in Europe and North America in the 20th century. Most of the examples were made between 1900 and 1960. However, there are a few examples of items made after 1960. It is important to note that since most of the examples are less than one hundred years old, they fall under the category of collectibles. Collectible fabrics are also known as vintage textiles. Technically, the term "antique" refers to items over one hundred years old.

The term "household linen" as used refers to items made for use in the house that are either (a) woven out of silk, linen, cotton or some combination of these fibers (such as cotton warp with linen weft) which may be embroidered or trimmed with lace or (b) made exclusively out of lace using silk, linen or cotton thread. We have tried to include examples of both very rare and more commonly found items. In addition, when possible, we have indicated items which have been and/or are being copied today in the Far East.

Writing this book was a labor of love. It was written to encourage collectors to acquire, maintain, and use fine examples of 20th century linens and lace - an area that we have long felt to be ignored and undervalued. Prices have been included in the hope that they will promote an active market by giving buyers and sellers a benchmark for pricing. It should be noted that prices in this book refer to items in excellent condition unless otherwise specified.

Many of the examples illustrated herein are from the authors' collections. Collectively, they represent over twenty years of searching in the United States, Canada, Europe, and South America.

Numerous examples pictured in this book are from museums, private collections, and dealers' collections and inventories. We have noted the sources for all our examples. Where possible, we have also indicated when and where items were made. Countries of origin are sometimes difficult to determine because lacemakers brought their skills with them when they emigrated. For instance, an Italian lacemaker who continued to make lace after she moved to the United States would make lace commonly associated with Italy. In cases like this, in the absence of information from the family of the lacemaker, we would identify the lace as Italian.

It is also extremely difficult to be very precise regarding dates when items were made. We have therefore given ranges such as "first quarter of the 20th century" when describing various items. "Turn of the century" is a term often used in the antique world. This typically means that the item in question could have been made anywhere between 1875 and 1925. However, when used in this book, "turn of the century" refers to the period 1890 to 1920. To the best of our ability, we have also tried to distinguish between handmade and machine-made examples.

1.1 *Date Made: First quarter of the 20th century*
Description: An Appenzell-type linen tablecloth with ten figural medallions of varying sizes showing five scenes of courting couples. Each of the five scenes is depicted twice. Appenzell-type linen tablecloths of this quality are extremely rare and highly collectible. Because Appenzell-type pieces were often made for trousseaus, courting couples are a common theme in figural Appenzell-type work. Note how the faces, hands, and legs of the figures are covered with tiny satin stitches. In addition, extensive sections of the tablecloth between the medallions are covered in buratto work. The only two other figural tablecloths of
this quality that we have seen also depict courting couples. Believe it or not, this tablecloth was purchased as part of a box lot at auction in 1994.

Measurements: Overall dimensions: 92"L x 70"W
Dimensions of largest medallion: 16"L x 12"W
Dimensions of smallest medallion: 8"L x 7"W
Height of tallest figure: 4.5"
Height of smallest figure: 3"
Collection of: Peggy Zalamea

Chapter 1

Appenzell and Appenzell-Type Embroidery

Appenzell embroidery was made in a small town called Appenzell which is located near the extreme northeastern corner of Switzerland near the German border. Although Appenzell is classified as embroidery, we have separated it from the chapter on embroidery for the following reasons:

1) We consider it to be the finest embroidery of the 20th century; and 2) There is very little documentation of Appenzell in existing literature on 20th century linens and lace.

We hope this chapter will inspire collectors and researchers alike. The time we have devoted to studying and collecting Appenzell has been fascinating for us.

This type of embroidery has been famous since 1780. It is whitework embroidery with linen thread on cotton, linen and, more rarely, silk. Unfortunately, there are no known examples of the early development of Appenzell; however, there is documentation on it.

Most Appenzell was produced in the home rather than in factories. The five hundred Swiss Franc bill in circulation from 1912 to 1955 shows a group of Appenzell ladies working beside a window in a home setting (photograph 1.2).

The embroidery industry in the eastern part of Switzerland peaked at the beginning of the 20th century. Some of the most beautiful examples of Appenzell were made at this time. Among the rarest pieces are those done in the workshop of the Swiss painter H.C. Ulrich. They can be identified because he placed his signature on them. We have included a photograph of a doily made in his shop in 1916 (photograph 1.3) as well as a closeup of his signature (photograph 1.4).

It is very difficult to identify 20th century Appenzell since similar work was done in Germany, France, and Majorca at the same time. Sources at the Cooper-Hewitt Museum have told us that the best way to identify it is by the small gold tag that was attached to each piece after it was made. Unfortunately, most of these tags were removed years ago. Therefore, when we cannot document that a piece was made in the town of Appenzell, Switzerland, we call it Appenzell-type.

In terms of 20th century Appenzell embroidery, the padded satinstitch is characteristic. Also, from 1915 to 1930, the drawn thread stitch was widely used. Many of the examples in this chapter reflect one or both of these techniques.

This chapter includes two examples of Appenzell we have been able to document. It also includes a duvet cover and matching sham of German origin (photograph 1.13) and a tablecloth and two napkins that were made in Majorca (photographs 1.26-1.30). The pieces from Majorca were given to Swiss merchant Otto Bischoff in May 1926 as a wedding gift.

Appenzell and Appenzell-type pieces, especially figural ones, are extremely difficult to find. We highly recommend that pieces of Appenzell and Appenzell-type embroidery be added to your collection. Prices have been rising swiftly over the last decade. The finest examples of Appenzell and Appenzell-type are some of the most expensive early 20th century household linens on the market today. However, it is still possible to find underpriced pieces.

Appenzell and Appenzell-type embroidery was done by machine as well as by hand. Interesting examples of floral and figural work done by machine are pictured in the book entitled *La Broderie Mecanique*, Paris, 1931, by Ernest Iklé.

1.2 Origin: Switzerland
Date Made: 1912-1955
Description: A five hundred Swiss Franc bill in circulation from 1912 to 1955, designed by the artist Eugene Burnand. The bill shows Appenzell ladies working at the window.
Photograph courtesy of: Textilmuseum mit Textilbibliothek, St. Gallen, Switzerland

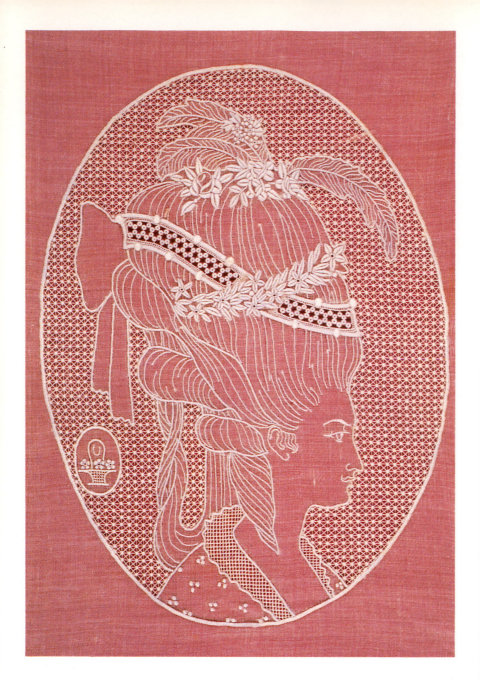

1.3 Origin: Appenzell, Switzerland
Date Made: 1916
Description: An Appenzell doily designed in the workshop of the painter
H.C. Ulrich, 1916, and embroidered by the women he employed there.
Photograph courtesy of: Textilmuseum mit Textilbibliothek, St. Gallen,
Switzerland

1.4 Detail with the signature of the artist, H.C. Ulrich. The signature is
a U in a basket with flowers.
Photograph courtesy of: Textilmuseum mit Textilbibliothek, St. Gallen,
Switzerland

1.5 *Date Made: First quarter of the 20th century*
Description: This Appenzell-type figural linen hand towel is superb.
Even the monogram is a work of art. The two cherubs in this towel are
exquisitely done in tiny satin stitches of the same quality as those seen in
the pair of pillowcases in photograph 1.6. The figural medallion is
surrounded with buratto work in a floral design. Buratto work is often
seen in the highest quality Appenzell and Appenzell-type work. This
towel is one of a pair. The other half of this pair is in the collection of
Kay Mertens.
Measurements: Overall dimensions: 32.5"L x 22"W
Dimensions of the medallion: 8"L x 6"W
Height of monogram: 3"
Collection of: Debra Bonito

1.6 *Date Made: First quarter of the 20th century*
Description: This Appenzell-type linen pillowcase is one of the finest
examples we have seen. It is one of a pair. To have the cherubs entirely
covered in tiny satin stitches is unusual. It is more typical to have a
raised outline around the edges of the figure and to define facial
features and clothing as seen in the tablecloth in photograph 1.8.
Although cherubs are a common theme in most types of early 20th

century lace, they are not common in Appenzell-type pieces. This pair of
pillowcases may not have been sold originally with a matching bed
sheet.
Measurements: Overall dimensions: 37"L x 23"W
Dimension of medallion: 6"L x 3.75"W
Height of tallest figure: 2.25"
Collection of: Elizabeth Scofield

1.7 *Detail of the medallion in photograph 1.6.*

1.8 *Date Made: First quarter of the 20th century*
Description: Round Appenzell-type tablecloth. This linen tablecloth has eight Art Noveau ladies on it. They form a circle divided by vases of flowers. Three of the ladies are identical to the one in this photograph. The additional four are similar. This piece is rare because of the subject matter and because it is very difficult to find round Appenzell-type tablecloths this size.
Measurements: Diameter: 50"
Dimensions of figures: 9"L x 2.5"W
Collection of: Elizabeth Scofield

1.9 *Date Made: First quarter of the 20th century*
Description: A figural Appenzell-type runner with a large center medallion depicting a gentleman climbing a fruit tree with two ladies observing him. At each end of the runner there is a smaller medallion showing a courting couple. The two smaller medallions are identical. This runner is one of a pair. The other half of this pair is in a private collection in California. The workmanship in this runner is very good but not as fine as the towel featured in photograph 1.5. Appenzell-type runners are extremely rare.
Measurements: Overall dimensions: 108"L x 11"W
Dimensions of the small medallions: 6.25"L x 7.50"W
Dimensions of the large center medallion: 8"L x 11"W
Height of the largest figure: 4.5"
Collection of: Debra Bonito

1.10 *Date Made: First quarter of the 20th century*
Description: Figural Appenzell-type pillowcase. The front of this piece is
almost entirely covered with buratto work and embroidery. The central
medallion depicts an antique-style scene of four ladies and a gentleman
in a drawing room. The figures are covered with small satin stitches of
excellent quality. This is the highest quality piece of Appenzell-type
embroidery in this chapter. The only piece we have seen of similar
quality is in the Musee des Arts Decorotifs in Paris.
Measurements: Overall dimensions: 19.5"L x 24"W
Dimensions of the central medallion: 6.25"L x 16"W
Height of the largest seated figure: 6.25"
Collection of: Debra Bonito

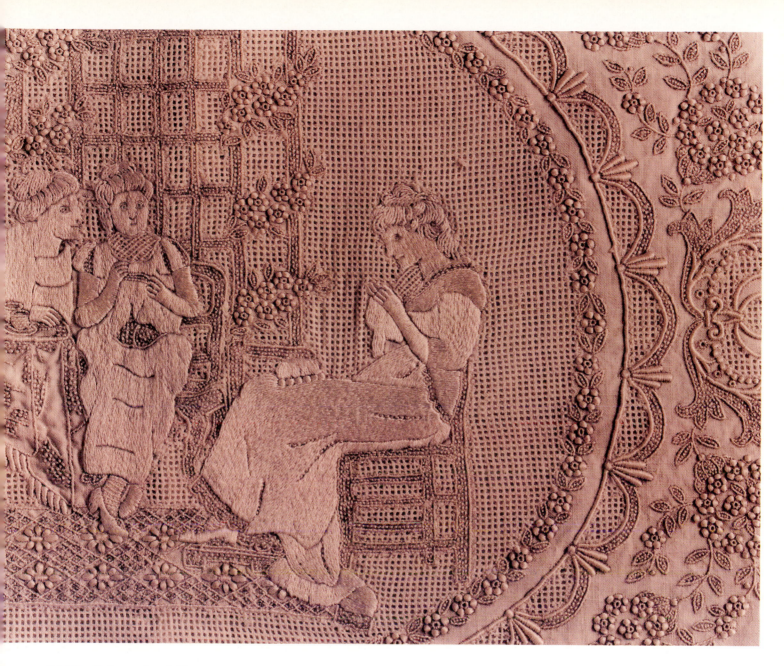

1.11 *Detail of central medallion.*

1.12 Date Made: *First quarter of the 20th century*
Description: Figural linen Appenzell-type handkerchief case. The satin stitching on the faces and hands of the lady and gentleman is very fine, and the detail on their clothing is excellent. This quality of workmanship is extremely rare.
Measurements: Overall dimensions: 19"L x 6.25"W
Height of figures: 6"
Collection of: Kay Mertens

1.13 *Date Made: First quarter of the 20th century*
Description: A figural Appenzell-type linen bed sheet with a matching
pillowcase, an Appenzell-type duvet cover, and a matching single sham.
The pillowcase is one of a pair. Although the workmanship in both sets is
very good, there are better examples in this chapter. The scenes on the
bed sheet and pillowcase depict courting couples. Both pieces bear the
monogram "APS". The duvet cover and single sham have never been
used. They still have the original paper labels from the store in Germany
where they were purchased in the 1930s for the first owner by his mother.
The owner subsequently fled to the U.S. to escape the Nazis. This duvet
cover and sham were among the possessions he brought with him. He
eventually sold the set to Kay Mertens, a well-known New York vintage
textile dealer, who then sold them to Peggy. Both the duvet and the sham
bear the monogram "B".
Measurements: Overall dimensions of the bedsheet: 100"L x 68.5"W
Diameter of the medallion in bed sheet: 9"
Overall dimensions of the pillowcases: 33.5"L x 2.3"W
Overall dimensions of the duvet cover: 96"L x 61.5"W
Overall dimensions of the single sham: 31.5"L x 31"W
Collection of: Peggy Zalamea

1.14 *Date Made: First quarter of the 20th century*
Description: Appenzell-type tablecloth and napkin. The linen napkin has a medallion of a cherub holding a garland of flowers. It is one of a set of eight napkins. The linen tablecloth has twelve large medallions. Two of the medallions are of a lady holding a parrot; two additional medallions are of a lady holding a bouquet of flowers with a butterfly at her side; and eight are identical to the cherub medallion. The workmanship in this tablecloth is not as fine as the tablecloth shown in photograph 1.1. However, it is difficult to find an Appenzell-type tablecloth with cherubs and matching napkins; therefore, we have classified this set as rare.

Measurements: Overall dimensions of the napkins: 22.5"W x 23.5"L
Dimensions of the medallion: 5.5"W x 8.5"L
Height of the cherub: 3.25"
Overall dimensions of the tablecloth: 72"W x 104"L
Dimensions of the medallions with cherubs: 12"L x 16"W
Dimensions of the medallions with ladies: 10"W x 7"L
Dimensions of the largest figure: 7"H x 4"W
Collection of: Elizabeth Scofield

1.15 *Two additional medallions in the tablecloth.*

1.16 *Date Made: First quarter of the 20th century*
Description: Linen Appenzell-type placemat. One of a set of six. The same figural scene is reflected on both ends of the placemat. The quality of workmanship is closer to that of the pillowcase in photo 1.6 and is clearly superior to that of the tea cloth in photograph 1.22. This is the second complete set of figural placemats we have seen. Sets of Appenzell-type placemats are expensive and many sets have been broken up over the years to make them more affordable for collectors. The dealer this set was purchased from had already sold two of the placemats by the time Liz spotted them.
Measurements: Overall dimensions: 16"L x 11"W
Dimensions of each medallion: 5"L x 4"W
Height of tallest figure: 2"
Collection of: Elizabeth Scofield

1.17 *Detail of the placemat's figural scene.*

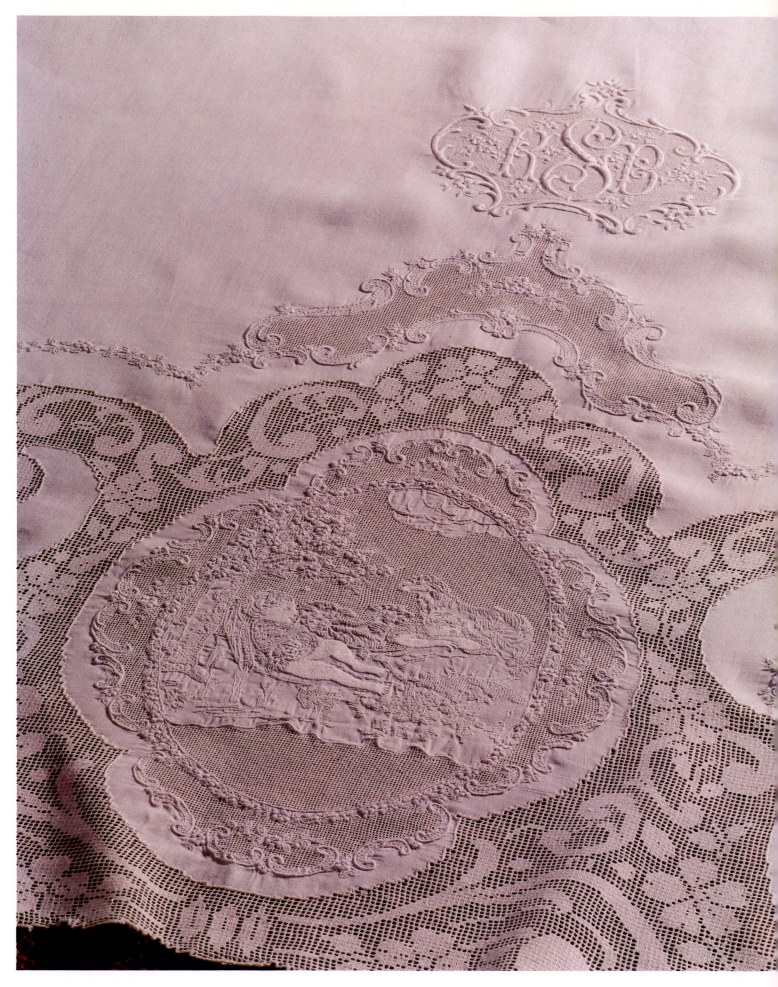

1.19 *Date Made: First quarter of the 20th century*
Description: Appenzell-type linen tray cover. The design of a bride and
groom indicates that this was probably a common trousseau piece. This
piece is average quality. There is minimal damage on the edges.
Measurements: Overall dimensions: 18"L x 11.5"W
Height of the figures: 4"
Collection of: Elizabeth Scofield

1.18 *Date Made: 1920-1926*
Description: Appenzell-type linen bed sheet. The workmanship on this
sheet is excellent. The design is intricate. The human figures (there are
two) are almost entirely covered with satin stitch. The monogram is one
of the finest we have ever seen. This sheet came with the pillowcase
shown in photograph 1.6. However, they may not be a set. The sheet and
the pillowcases were part of Kathryn B. Smith's (deceased) trousseau.
She was married in New York City on April 10, 1926.
Measurements: Overall dimensions: 118"L x 72"W
Dimensions of medallion: 11"L x 8.5"W
Collection of: Elizabeth Scofield

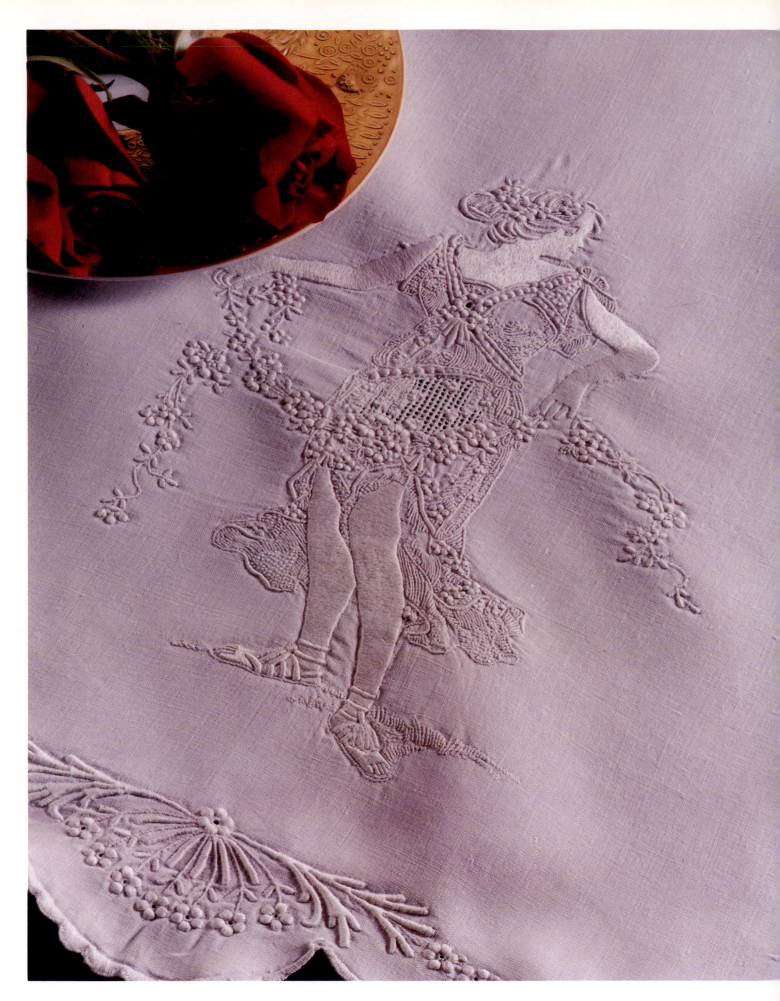

1.20 Date Made: First quarter of the 20th century
Description: A round linen Appenzell-type tablecloth with a scalloped
border. This cloth is adorned with four Art Nouveau female dancers,
whose bodies are covered in very fine satin stitch. Each of the dancers is
different. Vases of flowers seperate them. The subject matter is highly
unusual for Appenzell-type work. This piece is one of the best examples
shown in this book.
Measurements: Diameter: 30.25"
Height of the female figure: 7.5"
Height of the vase of flowers: 5.25"
Collection of: Debra Bonito

1.21 Vase of flowers on the tablecloth.

1.22 Date Made: First quarter of the 20th century
Description: An Appenzell-type square linen tea cloth with a medallion
of a courting couple on each of the four sides. Although there are four
medallions, there are only two different scenes, each of which is
repeated twice.
Measurements: Overall dimensions: 38.5" square
Dimensions of each medallion: 8" square
Average height of figures: 4.5"
Collection of: Elizabeth Scofield

1.23 *The other medallion on the tea cloth.*

1.24 Origin: *Appenzell, Switzerland*
Date Made: *First quarter of the 20th century*
Description: *A richly embroidered cushion cover with padded
satin stiches and drawnwork.*
Photograph courtesy of:
*Textilmuseum mit
Textilbibliothek, St. Gallen,
Switzerland*

1.25 *Detail of the cushion cover.*

1.26 Origin: Majorca
Date Made: 1926
Description: A figural
Appenzell-type napkin which
matches the tablecloth in
photograph 1.28. The subject
matter is a visualization from
Don Quixote. This napkin is
excellent quality.
Photograph courtesy of:
Textilmuseum mit
Textilbibliothek, St. Gallen,
Switzerland.

1.27 Origin: Majorca
Date Made: 1926
Description: A figural
Appenzell-type napkin which
matches the tablecloth in
photograph 1.28 and the napkin
in photograph 1.26. This napkin
is excellent quality.
Photograph courtesy of:
Textilmuseum mit
Textilbibliothek, St. Gallen,
Switzerland.

1.28 Origin: Majorca
Date Made: 1926
Description: An Appenzell-type
tablecloth depicting a visualization from Don Quixote. This
piece and its matching napkins
(photographs 1.26 and 1.27) are
of excellent quality and the
subject matter is very rare.
Photograph courtesy of:
Textilmuseum mit
Textilbibliothek, St. Gallen,
Switzerland.

1.29 and 1.30 Detail of scenes from the tablecloth in photograph 1.28.

2.1 *Date Made: First quarter of the 20th century*
Description: *Machine-made net curtains with linen Battenberg lace borders. The machine-made tape was joined together by hand. This type of curtain was made in the Victorian era and into the first quarter of the 20th century. The quality of machine-made net as well as the lace varied widely in this type of curtain. The nets range from flimsy to very sturdy. The net in this set falls into the latter category. The Battenberg lace border is excellent quality. The thread covering the rings is densely packed unlike many new pieces which either do not have rings or have rings with very skimpy thread that unravels very easily. In addition, the length of these curtains is at least one hundred inches long which makes them considerably more valuable than shorter curtains of comparable quality. It is much easier to shorten a curtain than to lengthen it.*
Measurements: Overall dimensions of each panel: 101"L X 34"W
Width of lace at the bottom: 17"
Collection of: Peggy Zalamea

Chapter 2

Battenberg and Other Tape Laces

Battenberg is the best known modern tape lace, and many dealers and collectors use the name Battenberg as a generic term meant to cover most types of tape lace. Battenberg was originally produced in Belgium and is now made all over the world. In the early 1900s, making Battenberg was a favorite pastime. It could be made quickly when compared to other types of lace.

Tape laces derive their name from the fact that the main part of their design is constructed by a continuous tape. The tape is made by hand or machine and is twisted and stitched into place, then joined by bobbin-made bars or needlepoint stitches. Many early 20th century Battenberg pieces include rings that were used as flower centers or to form grape clusters. These rings could be purchased at the same stores that sold ready made tape. The Butterick Publishing Company's book on Battenberg and Other Tape Laces uses the following names for different types of braids (tapes) used in 20th century tape lace making:

Battenberg
Bruge
Russian
Flemish
Cluny
Honiton
Duchesse
Point Lace
Marie Antoinette

For the purposes of this book, we will refer to all of the above as Battenberg tape.

At first glance, some bobbin laces such as Cantu appear to be tape laces. However, closer examination of these bobbin laces will show that the connecting bars or brides are interwoven with the rest of the piece and were not added later as is the case with tape lace. In addition, since lace tapes are made on a straight line and not on a curve, there is considerable puckering or folding of the material in the corners of pieces made out of tape lace. Bobbin lace pieces, on the other hand, have smoothly rounded corners.

Some of the older Battenberg as well as other tape laces are considered quite collectible. Battenberg and other tape laces are usually used for borders and/or centers for doilies, tablecloths, curtains, and bed covers. They are more rarely used to make entire pieces. Large pieces such as bed covers or tablecloths seating at least eight are very rare.

Dealers in the United States report that Battenberg is the most popular lace on the market today. In Toronto, Battenberg pieces are usually the first to go at antique shows where Peggy shows her merchandise. At one show she saw a forty inch round Battenberg lace and linen tea cloth sell for $220.00 Canadian, while a rectangular needle lace tablecloth that seated six sold for $175.00 Canadian. Both pieces were in excellent condition. This is a classic example of fashion affecting price. The needle lace tablecloth required considerably more time to make and is much more difficult to find. It should have commanded a higher price.

A large quantity of Battenberg lace is being produced in China today, some of which is being sold as old Battenberg in various flea markets around the country. There is a difference in the quality of old versus new Battenberg with a corresponding difference in price. Compared to many other household linens of comparable quality, Battenberg pieces are quite expensive. Nevertheless, strong demand continues to push prices of older Battenberg higher.

2.2 Origin: Belgium

Date Made: Turn of the century

Description: A Battenberg lace bed cover made of linen thread. Note
the intricacy of the design, which is much more interesting than that of
pieces made after the 1950s. Bed covers made entirely of Battenberg or
any other kind of lace are rare. This piece is extremely rare because it is
one of a pair. When used in larger pieces, tape laces were more
commonly used as borders or insertions. The measurements given here
are for the bed cover in its current state. A previous owner had reduced
the width of the piece by folding four inches under on either side and
stitching the excess lace flat. If these stitches were unpicked, the piece
would be eight inches wider than the measurement indicated below.
This piece has excellent workmanship.

Measurements: Overall dimensions: 102"L X 75"W

Collection of: Peggy Zalamea

2.3 Date Made: Turn of the century
Description: *A square tape lace tablecloth fashioned from bobbin made tape with an eight pointed star in the center. The star's points are a leaf motif, the center is a circle of laurel leaves. The cloth is connected with a series of elaborate brides. The border is a "fringe" resembling the star points.*
Measurements: *Overall dimensions: 93" square*
Collection of: *Paley Design Center, Philadelphia College of Textiles and Science*

2.4 *Date made (tea cloth): Turn of the century*
Date made (coasters): Second half of the 20th century
Description: A round tea cloth with a cotton drawnwork center
surrounded by Battenberg lace together with a set of four cotton
Battenberg lace coasters. This tea cloth is better quality than the runner
(photograph 2.7) but is not the high quality of the curtains or the bed
covers shown elsewhere in this chapter. The coasters are very typical of
Battenberg pieces being made today. Note the absence of rings and the
simple, unimaginative design. Neither piece is particularly collectible.
Both are easy to find. The tea cloth is relatively expensive but the
coasters are very affordable.
Measurements: Diameter of tea cloth: 44"
Diameter of coasters: 6"
Collection of: Peggy Zalamea

2.5 Date Made: First half of the 20th century
Description: A cotton tablecloth with a Battenberg lace border and
insertions. The tablecloth has twleve matching napkins, as seen in
photograph 2.6. All the pieces in the set have an embroidered initial "L".
The workmanship is good. It is difficult to find either large Battenberg
tablecloths or sets of eight or more Battenberg lace napkins. For both
these reasons, this set is expensive.
Measurements: Overall dimensions of tablecloth: 106"L X 72"W
Overall dimensions of napkins: 15.25" X 16"
Collection of: Peggy Zalamea

2.6 Napkin that matches the tablecloth in photograph 2.5.

2.7 Date Made: *First half of the 20th century*
Description: *A runner consisting of four cotton drawnwork squares*
bordered by Battenberg lace. The workmanship is average, and the
design is rather uninspired. This runner is not the quality of the curtain
and pair of bed covers shown elsewhere in this chapter. This item is easy
to find; however, it is expensive because Battenberg is very collectible.
Measurements: *Overall dimensions: 68"L X 16.25"W*
Collection of: *Peggy Zalamea*

Bobbin lace is also known as pillow lace because it is made on a firm pillow to which a pricked-out pattern is attached. Small rods three to six inches in length called bobbins carry numerous threads over the pattern and each twist of the bobbins is held in place by a pin. Up until the latter part of the 16th century, fish bones were often used to make the pins and bobbins used to form the lace. As a result, bobbin lace is also known as bone lace in England. A pillow with bobbin lace being made on it is pictured in photgraph 3.1.

As discussed in Chapter II, bobbin lace often resembles tape lace but is easily distinguished from tape lace by three things:

1) The width of the tape can change from section to section in the same piece of bobbin lace. This is impossible in tape lace.

2) Bobbin lace has smoothly rounded corners, whereas tape laces have puckered or folded corners.

3) Connecting stitches or brides in bobbin lace are incorporated into the piece when it is being made unlike tape lace where they are added after the tapes are made.

Most bobbin lace has a loosely woven, airy look to it. The main exception to this is a Venetian bobbin lace called Cantu, which was developed in the 19th century and continues to be made today. Cantu is very tightly woven and is often mistaken for tape lace. The tablecloth featured in photograph 3.16 is an excellent example of Cantu lace.

Bobbin lace has been used to create all types of household linens. It is used for edging, insertion pieces, and to make whole pieces. Handmade bobbin lace pieces are often applied to machine-made nets to make cushion covers and edging. Twentieth century bobbin lace placemats and tablecloths were typically done in Cantu as well as other types of bobbin lace.

European bobbin lace, particularly figural examples, is very collectible. Twentieth century figural Cantu pieces are commanding some of the highest prices in the market today. Sets of six or more figural placemats are quite rare. They are even rarer and more valuable when they have matching napkins and runners. Prices of complete sets often exceed that of tablecloths seating the same number of people. A set of twelve placemats with a figural Cantu lace border, matching napkins, and runner was advertised for sale in the *Lace Collector Newsletter*, Fall, 1991, at an asking price of $1,450.00.

Bobbin lace continues to be made in Europe and North America. The Chinese are also producing good copies of Western bobbin lace today. Linen, silk, and cotton threads have all been used to produce bobbin lace. Chinese copies are not considered collectible.

3.1 Origin of tablecloth: China
Date: First half of the 20th century
Description: A ruffled pillow showing the technique of making bobbin lace with a piece of lace in progress, and a cotton bobbin lace tablecloth. The pillow has a piece of vellum with pins on it. There are wooden bobbins with yarns wound tightly hanging from it. The holes in the vellum hold the pins to form the design of the lace. The tablecloth is made entirely of this type of bobbin lace. We do not see large pieces made entirely of bobbin lace very often; however, prices remain low because this type of piece does not seem to be in great demand.
Measurements: Overall dimensions of tablecloth: 81"L x 59"W
Overall dimensions of pillow: 23.5"L x 23"W
Tablecloth, collection of: Elizabeth Scofield
Pillow, collection of: The Paley Design Center, Philadelphia College of Textiles and Science,
Gift of: Mrs. Stanley W. Root, Jr.

3.2 *Date: First quarter of the 20th century*
Description: Linen tea cloth with eight bobbin lace insertions,
drawnwork, and a bobbin lace border. Four of the insertions are
figural. Two of them depict ships, and two depict windmills. The subject
matter of this cloth is interesting and makes it collectible.
Measurements: Overall dimensions (including fringe): 39" square
Dimensions of the large insertions: 4.25" square
Dimensions of the small insertions: 2"L x 4"W
Width of the border: varies from 3.5" to 5"
Collection of: Elizabeth Scofield

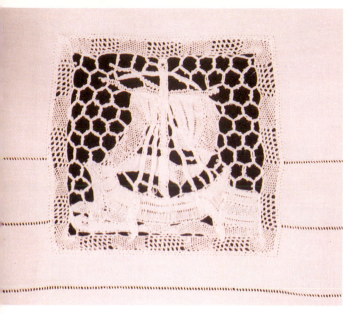

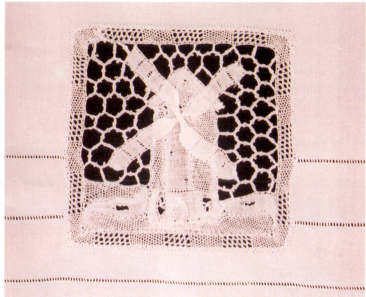

3.3 *Detail of one of the figural insertions.*

3.4 *Detail of one of the figural insertions.*

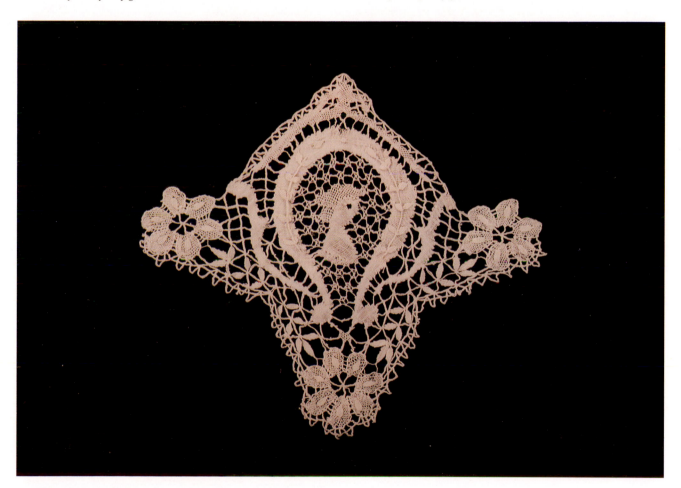

3.5 *Date Made: First quarter of the 20th century*
Description: This linen, figural, bobbin lace insertion piece is an
unusual shape. Squares, triangles, ovals, and circles are more typical
shapes for insertion pieces. This appears to have been made for use as
the corner edge on a larger piece. Small, interesting pieces like this are
very popular for framing.
Measurements: Overall dimensions: 12"L x 13.5"W
Collection of: Peggy Zalamea

3.6 *Date Made: First half of the 20th century*
Description: A linen tablecloth with a wide bobbin lace border and
bobbin lace insertions. This type of tablecloth is becoming difficult to
find.
Measurements: Diameter (including border): 37"
Width of lace border: varies from 5" to 8.25"
Dimensions of largest insertion: 3.25"L x 2.75"W
Collection of: Elizabeth Scofield

3.7 *Detail*

3.8 *Date Made: First half of the 20th century*
Description: A linen tea cloth with drawnwork and a wide bobbin lace border. The workmanship in this piece is excellent.
Measurements: Overall dimensions (including border): 25" square
Width of the lace border: 7.5"
Collection of: Elizabeth Scofield

3.9 *Detail*

3.10 *Date Made: First half of the 20th century*
Description: A round linen tablecloth with bobbin lace insertions and a
bobbin lace border. There are five figural insertions surrounded by
cutwork and embroidery on the cloth. Each insertion depicts a musician
playing an instrument. The medallions are shown in detail. The bobbin
lace insertions are excellent quality. The border of the cloth is machine-
made; however, it is very collectible because of its subject matter.
Measurements: Diameter (including the fringe): 61"
Dimensions of the insertions: 7.5"L x 4.25"W
Height of the largest figure: 4.75"
Width of fringe: varies from 3.5" to 4.5"
Collection of: Anna Burns

3.11 *Detail*

3.12 *Detail*

3.13 *Detail*

3.14 *Detail*

3.15 *Detail*

3.16 *Origin: Venice, Italy*

Date Made: First quarter of the 20th century

Description: This figural, Cantu bobbin lace tablecloth is one of the finest examples of this type of lace we have ever seen. There are sixty-one birds in this piece. Birds are not a common theme in most types of needle and bobbin lace; however, Cantu lace seems to be an exception. As previously mentioned, birds have appeared in Cantu lace placemats, napkins, and runners. The workmanship in this tablecloth is exquisite. Although Cantu lace is still made today in Venice and has been extensively copied in China, pieces of this size are very rare. The workmanship in Chinese copies is quite good; however, the Chinese designs are very simple and to date we have not seen any figural copies.

The four cotton napkins bordered by Cantu bobbin lace shown here are part of a set of twenty-four. They were not purchased with this tablecloth. A set of twenty-four napkins is very rare and highly sought after by many collectors.

Measurements: Overall dimensions of the tablecloth: 132"L x 82"W

Dimensions of largest bird: 7.25"H x 1.50"W

Dimensions of largest bird in nest: 4.75"L x 4"W

Dimensions of nest: 2.75"L x 3.75"W

Overall dimensions of napkins: 21" square

Tablecloth, collection of: Elizabeth Scofield and Peggy Zalamea

Napkins, collection of: Peggy Zalamea

3.17 *Detail*

3.18 Origin: Flemish
Date Made: 1935 - 1945
Description: A cotton tray cover and doily bordered in figural bobbin lace. There are sixteen ducks in the border of the tray cover and eight swans in the border of the doily. These pieces are very good quality. Please note that machine-made copies of this type of lace were made.
Measurements: Overall dimensions of the tray cover: 13"L x 17"W
Overall dimensions of the doily: 8"L x 11"W
Collection`of: Elizabeth Scofield

3.19 Date Made: First quarter of the 20th century
Description: Figural, bobbin lace placemat depicting an angel playing a trumpet. This type of piece is often framed. It is collectible because of its subject matter.
Measurements: Overall dimensions: 9"L x 18"W
Dimensions of angel: 7.5"L x 12"W
Collection of: Elizabeth Scofield

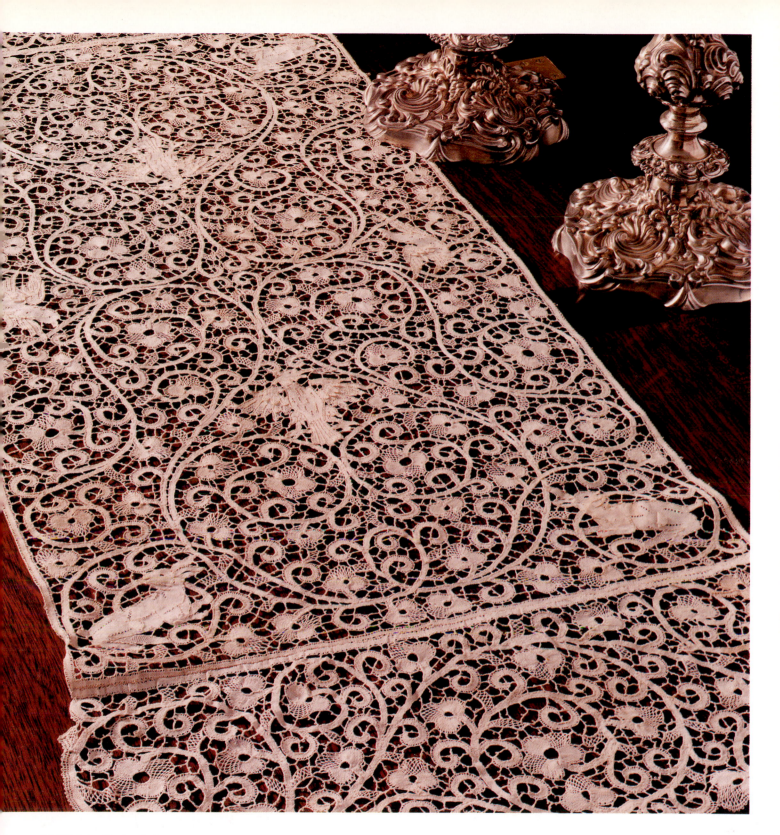

3.20 Origin: *Venice, Italy*
Date Made: *First quarter of the 20th century*
Description: *Figural, Cantu bobbin lace runner. This is similar in theme
and quality to the workmanship in the tablecloth in photograph 3.17.
There are eight animals-four birds and four deer on the runner. The
deer were made separately and then applied to the piece. This piece is
highly collectible.*
Measurements: *Overall dimensions: 38"L x 14"W*
Dimensions of largest figure: 3.25"L x 3.25"W
Collection of: *Peggy Zalamea*

3.21 Origin: *Venice, Italy*
Date Made: First half of the 20th century
Description: Figural, Cantu bobbin lace placemat and matching cotton
napkin. The placemat and napkin are from a set of twelve. Sets of this
size are difficult to find. Placemats with this type of lace are still made
today. However, they are usually not figural and are more expensive
than this set. This set is very collectible.
Measurements: Overall dimensions of placemats: 15"L x 9.75"W
Overall dimensions of napkin: 16"square
Collection of: Suthira Zalamea

3.22 Date Made: First quarter of the 20th century

Description: One panel of a pair of machine net and bobbin lace curtains. The bobbin lace border is made with linen thread and the net is machine-made. The workmanship is of good quality. The depth of the lace border and the overall design make this piece attractive and interesting. The main drawback to this piece is its length. It is very short particularly when compared to other machine net and lace examples in this book. While this piece is still a good addition to any collection, the length makes it less desirable than the pair of curtains in Chapter Two. Although the machine-made net is sturdy, one panel has two or three minor tears where the net joins the lace border. Since the lace is in excellent condition and the tears in the net are only apparent if one examined them very carefully, we consider the condition of these curtains to be excellent. When pricing curtains of this type, you should factor in the cost of repairing or replacing the damaged areas in cases where there is highly visible and/or major damage. However, as long as the lace is in perfect condition, the cost to repair should be minor and you should not expect a huge discount.

Measurements: Overall dimensions of each panel including fringe: 75"L x 67"W

Width of lace at highest point: 37.5"

Height of fringe: 12"

Collection of : Peggy Zalamea

3.23 Date Made: First quarter of the 20th century
Description: A sleigh bed cover with a bobbin lace border on two sides
and a bobbin lace insertion in the center.   The eight small insertions are
identical and appear to be reptiles. The larger insertion depicts two
cherubs.
Measurements: Overall dimensions (excluding fringe): 71.5"L x 54"W
Dimensions of small insertions: 4.5"L x 4.5"W
Dimensions of large insertion: 13.5"L x 8.25" W
Height of cherubs: 7"
Width of fringe: 4.5"
Collection of: Anna Burns

3.24 *Origin: Venice, Italy*
Date Made: First quarter of the 20th century
*Description: A three piece Venetian Cantu bobbin lace antimacassar
set. This lace is often mistaken for tape lace. Antimacassar sets were
very popular in Victorian times and in the first half of the 20th century.
It is difficult to find complete sets. Headrests are more common than
armrests.*
Measurements: Overall dimensions of the headrest: 11"L x 16"W
Overall dimensions of armrest: 11"L x 7"W
Collection of: Peggy Zalamea

3.25 Date Made: First half of the 20th century
Description: Organdy cocktail napkin with a figural, bobbin lace insertion. This napkin is one in a set of twelve. The combination of organdy and bobbin lace is unusual.
Measurements: Overall dimensions: 5.25"L x 7.75"W
Dimensions of insertion: 1.50" square
Collection of: Elizabeth Scofield

3.26 Origin: Venice, Italy
Date Made: First half of the 20th century
Description: A Venetian Cantu figural bobbin lace runner, matching figural placemat, and three matching napkins. These pieces are from a set which includes twelve napkins, twelve placemats, and the runner shown here. The cutwork cotton centers and the theme of a seated lady with a harp make this set atypical. Most Cantu lace pieces are made entirely of lace. When they are figural, cherubs are the most common theme. This set is highly collectible.
Measurements: Overall dimensions of runner: 52"L x 17"W
Dimensions of largest figure: 4.875"H x 2.78"W
Overall dimensions of placemats: 17.5"L x 11.5"W

3.27 Origin: *Various countries described below*

Date Made: *First half of the 20th century*

Description: *The five doilies show a wide variety of bobbin laces. The square doily is silk maltese lace and is one of a set of five. The coarsest looking ecru doily is made with linen thread. The type of lace used in this doily was often used with machine-made net to make curtains and bed covers in the late 19th and early 20th Centuries. The doily with the brown silk center was made in France and is one of a set of twelve. The cotton tape lace border on this doily looks very similar to the bobbin lace insertion in the hand towel. It was included in this photograph for comparison purposes. Note the puckering and the folding of the tape at the corners on the doily versus the smooth, rounder curves of the bobbin insertion. The doily with the white linen center in the shape of an "X" has a linen, bobbin lace border. It is one of a set of six. The white doily made entirely of cotton bobbin lace is one of a set of ten made in China. With the exception of the French silk set, all these doilies are easy to find*

individually or in sets of four or more. The linen runner with a linen bobbin lace border is easy to find at an affordable price. The bobbin lace insertion in the linen towel is a Chinese copy of Venetian Cantu lace. It is decorative and in great demand but still readily affordable. The linen napkin with a figural, bobbin lace corner is one of a set of four. The figural corner is very unusual and makes this set of napkins quite collectible. This set would be more valuable if there were at least eight napkins.

Measurements: *Overall dimensions of runner: 51"L x 18.5"W*

Overall dimensions of towel: 20.25"L x 16.5"W

Overall dimensions of napkin: 15.5"L x 15"W

Height of figure in napkin: .75"

Diameter of largest doily: 8.875"

Overall dimensions of smallest doily: 5"L x 5.25"W

Collection of: *Peggy Zalamea*

4.1 *Date Made: First quarter of the 20th century*
Description: A blue moiré, machine embroidered, figural bed cover
with fifty cherubs. This is one of the finest examples of 20th century
machine embroidery we have seen. Although machine embroidery is
generally less desirable than hand embroidery, the quality of this piece
makes it highly desirable.
Measurements: Overall dimensions excluding fringe: 64"L x 96"W
Width of the fringe: 6"
Height of each cherub: 5.5"
Collection of: Peggy Zalamea

Chapter 4

Chemical Lace and Other Machine Laces

Chemical Lace

Chemical lace, also known as burned lace, was invented in 1883 as an inexpensive imitation of handmade lace. Initially, machine embroidery was done in cotton thread on a silk background. The silk was then dissolved in chemicals, such as chlorine, leaving only the cotton lace. Currently, there are at least two methods used in making chemical lace. It is either done on an acetate rayon background, which dissolves in acetone, or on cotton fabric pretreated with acid so that it will readily dissolve in hot air or hot water. Chemical lace is easily distinguishable from handmade lace. Unlike handmade lace, chemical lace uses only one stitch--a zigzag lock stitch. It is characterized by uneven stitches that look as if they are about to unravel at any moment.

Chemical lace was commonly used as edging on small cotton or linen doilies and more rarely on runners, tea cloths, hand towels, napkins, placemats, pillowcases, and bed sheets. Placemats were also made entirely from this lace. We have not seen any tablecloths, placemats, or bed covers made exclusively of chemical lace. One of the largest examples of 20th century figural chemical lace we have seen is pictured in photograph 4.10.

Early 20th century chemical lace pieces, especially figural examples, are becoming very collectible. Pieces in excellent condition are becoming scarce for a number of reasons. In handmade needle lace, it is very easy to reattach the brides when they come loose. Unfortunately, chemical lace brides are quite difficult to reattach because they have a strong tendency to unravel once they become detached. The brides in chemical lace are quite fragile and become detached with annoying frequency. Most of the early 20th century pieces we have seen are too fragile for everyday use. They are also difficult to wash. Pieces that appear to be in excellent condition often fall apart when soaked. Do not under any circumstances attempt to wash these pieces in a washing machine! We recommend that you frame your chemical lace pieces.

Machine-Made Lace

The first machine-made nets were produced in the 1760s. The early efforts resembled hand-knitting. Bobbin machine net was the next to emerge in the early 1800's followed soon after by filet machine net, machine-made lace and machine embroidery in that order. Nineteenth century machine-made reproductions of handmade lace were so good that it can be difficult to distinguish between the two.

One of the most famous American machine lace companies of the 20th century is The Quaker Lace Company which made the wonderful figural tablecloth called *Washington Crossing the Delaware*. Large figural machine lace pieces made by the Quaker Lace Company as well as other manufacturers in the first half of the 20th century are becoming collectible. They were quite expensive at the time they were made, so there are very few available in today's market. Some of the more intricate, smaller figural pieces are also quite desirable as additions to a collection.

Machine Embroidery

Machine embroidery is done on both machine net as well as woven textiles. Machine embroidery on machine net is much more common than hand embroidery on machine net in the 20th century. Machine embroidery is distinguishable from hand embroidery by the regularity of the stitches. It should be noted that this is not true of some of the earliest examples of machine embroidery where the stitches could be quite uneven. Another way to distinguish between 20th century machine and hand embroidery is that the point at which the passing thread moves from one part of the design to another is always the same in each repeat in machine embroidery. In addition, there are the same number of stitches in each repeat which would be nearly impossible in hand embroidery. Finally, there is an absence of knots.

Machine embroidery continues to be made in large quantities today and, with few exceptions, is not considered highly collectible. One of the finest examples of 20th century machine embroidery we have seen is pictured in photograph 4.1. This piece is an exception; it is highly collectible.

4.2 *Origin: U.S.A.*
Date Made: Third quarter of the 20th century
Description: This pair of curtains consists of machine chain stitch on handkerchief linen. It is one of a set of four pairs. The chain stitch floral pattern is quite common. Single pairs of this type are easy to find and relatively inexpensive. Sets of three or more matching pairs are slightly more difficult to find.
Measurements: Overall dimensions of each panel (with pleats at top): 87"L x 40"W
Collection of: Peggy Zalamea

4.3 *Date Made: First quarter of the 20th century*
Description: A figural, machine-made bobbin lace sham made with cotton thread. Sixteen identical panels of a lady in 19th century costume were joined together by hand and then bordered by machine-made bobbin lace. This lace is excellent quality. If you are interested in machine-made lace pieces for your collection, a piece of this quality would be a good one to add.
Measurements: Overall dimensions: 35"L x 18"W
Collection of: Peggy Zalamea

4.4 *Date Made: First half of the 20th century*
*Description: A cotton pillow with figural machine-made lace insertions
and fringe. The pillow has four small insertions and a large one. The
four small insertions have a cherub on each of them. The large insertion
has six cherubs on it. This piece is collectible because of its subject
matter. Figural machine-made, filet lace pieces are easy to find at
affordable prices.*
Measurements: Overall dimensions: 14"L x 17.5"W
Dimensions of large insertions: 13.5"L x 6"W
Dimensions of small insertions: 3"L x 4.5"W
Collection of: Elizabeth Scofield

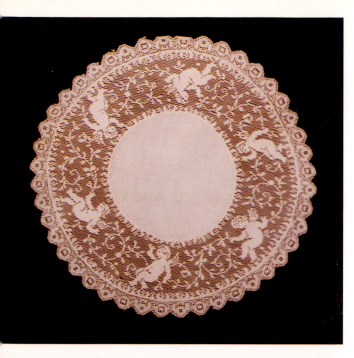

4.5 *Date Made: First half of the 20th century*
Description: A round linen doily with a wide machine-made filet lace border. The border is figural and depicts six cherubs in a circle. This piece is collectible because of its subject matter.
Measurements: Diameter: 11"
Width of border: 3"
Collection of: Elizabeth Scofield

4.6 *Date Made: First quarter of the 20th century*
Description: A chemical lace tray cover with a figural border. The border has twelve figures on it. This piece is in excellent condition. Figural chemical lace pieces are becoming difficult to find especially when they are in excellent condition.
Measurements: Overall dimensions: 13.25"L x 20"W
Dimensions of the largest figure: 2"L x 3.5"W
Collection of: Elizabeth Scofield

4.7 *Detail of photograph 4.6.*

4.8 *Date Made: First quarter of the 20th century*
Description: A chemical lace placemat. The placemat has ten figures on the border. The male figure seen in this photograph appears in each of the four corners; and the female appears in the center of the left and right borders. In addition, there are two female figures on both the top and bottom borders.
Measurements: Overall dimensions: 12"L x 17.5"W
Dimensions of largest figure: 3"L x 1.5"W
Collection of: Elizabeth Scofield

4.9 *Date Made: Second quarter of the 20th century*
Description: A machine-made tablecloth consisting of one hundred and twenty-one circles of lace. This cloth resembles handmade bobbin lace.
Measurements: Overall dimensions: 70" square
Collection of: Elizabeth Scofield

4.10 Origin: *U.S.A.*
Date Made: *First quarter of the 20th century*
Description: *A round linen tablecloth with figural chemical lace insertions and border. This is one of the largest figural chemical lace pieces we have seen to date. It has thirty-six figures and is in excellent condition. As discussed earlier, figural chemical lace pieces are becoming very collectible.*
Measurements: *Diameter: 50"*
Dimensions of largest figure: *4.5"H x 7"W*
Collection of: *Peggy Zalamea*

4.11 *Date Made: First half of the 20th century*
Description: A linen runner with a figural, chemical lace border, a rectangular chemical lace placemat and a French machine-made lace oval placemat. Of these pieces, the runner is the most collectible. The runner has eight figures on it.
Measurements: Overall dimensions of runner: 35"L x 17"W
Overall dimensions of rectangular placemat: 16.5"L x 11"W
Overall dimensions of oval placemat: 13.25"L x 9"W
First two pieces, collection of: Peggy Zalamea
Oval placemat, collection of: Elizabeth Scofield

4.12 Origin: *France*
Date Made: *Second quarter of the 20th century*
Description: *A machine-made tablecloth and cusion cover. The cloth
has a label that reads "Hand Run Alençon". It was made in France. The
cushion cover is one of a pair. It is machine-made with a scalloped
border and has a vase of flowers in the center.*
Measurements: *Overall dimensions of tablecloth: 42.5" square*
Overall dimensions of cushion cover: 16.5"L x 22"W
Collection of: *Elizabeth Scofield*

4.13 *Date made: First half of the 20th century*
*Description: A machine-made curtain panel. This panel was made to
resemble a linen curtain with filet lace insertions. From top to bottom,
the curtain has a large panel of flowers and garlands, a medallion with
four cherubs, a row of squares and octagons, and a row of baskets. The
bottom is scalloped with fringe sewn on it. The panel is one of a pair.
Measurements: Overall dimensions: 77.5"L x 37"W
Width of fringe: 2"
Collection of: Elizabeth Scofield*

4.14 Date Made: *Second half of the 20th century*
Description: *A machine-made bed cover and two pieces from a four piece dresser set. This set is unusual because it is made in two colors- ecru and pink.*
Measurements: *Overall dimensions of bed cover: 98"L x 88"W*
Overall dimension of dresser scarf: 18.5"L x 39"W
Collection of: *Elizabeth Scofield*

Different kinds of lace and embroidery were often used in the same piece. In addition, machine lace was often combined with handmade lace. In the latter instance, the intent was usually to produce a more affordable piece.

There are probably an infinite number of combinations possible. However, some combinations are consistently used. Some of the more common combinations are:

1) primarily cutwork with needle lace and/or other filet lace insertions and/or borders (photograph 5.10);

2) fagoting with bobbin or needle lace borders and/or insertions (photograph 5.17);

3) machine net with handmade bobbin or needle lace appliqué or insertions (photograph 5.24);

4) embroidery with bobbin or needle lace borders and/or insertions (photograph 5.22).

The ultimate form of combination lace is Normandy lace, also known as patchwork lace or lace samplers, which is highly collectible. Normandy lace is basically a crazy quilt made up of many different scraps of lace joined together in a discernable pattern. It can contain both machine and handmade lace. Normandy lace can be found in the forms of doilies, runners, cushion covers, tablecloths, and twin or full size bed covers (photograph 5.15). Large tablecloths and pairs of bed covers are more unusual. Normandy lace pieces, as a general rule, are in great demand and are quite expensive. They are becoming difficult to find in good condition.

Medium-size, rectangular cutwork tablecloths consisting of linen or cotton cutwork with non-figural inserts of filet lace or *point de venise* and filet lace borders are quite common. These tablecloths with matching napkins are slightly harder to find. Large round tablecloths with this combination of lace and embroidery are very rare, as are rectangular banquet size tablecloths with or without matching napkins. Figural tablecloths of all sizes with this same combination of cutwork and lace are also scarce. The latter three types command premium prices.

Cutwork table linen with needle lace or bobbin lace borders are harder to find than those with filet lace borders. In particular, sets of twelve linen cutwork dinner napkins with needle lace borders and inserts are rare.

5.1 Origin: Italy
Date Made: Turn of the century
Description: A white, cotton, square tablecloth consisting of alternating squares and rectangles of cutwork and embroidery and filet lace. The cloth has twenty-five figural, filet insertions with a scalloped filet border. The four corner filet squares have the names Appollo, Forche, Flora and Minerva on them.
Measurements: Overall Dimensions: 40" square
Dimensions of large filet insertions: 7.5" square
Dimensions of the small filet insertions: 3.5" square
Dimensions of cutwork: 7.25"L x 3.5"W
Collection of: The Paley Design Center,
Philadelphia College of Textiles and Science
Gift of: Mr. and Mrs. Henry Weis

5.2 Origin: China
Date Made: Second half of the 20th century
Description: A tablecloth with two matching napkins. The napkins are
from a set of eight. The tablecloth consists of alternating squares of filet
lace and embroidery and is bordered in scalloped filet lace with flowers.
The embroidered squares have drawnwork and satin-stitch. Tablecloths
with this alternating pattern are known as Army/Navy cloths. The
napkins have embroidery in one corner and a filet lace border.

Tablecloths with this same design were also made with multi-colored
embroidery in China. These Chinese tablecloths are plentiful and very
inexpensive. European Army/Navy cloths such as the one shown in
photograph no. 5.1 are hard to find and very collectible.
Measurements: Overall dimensions of tablecloth: 104"L x 68"W
Overall dimensions of napkin: 24" square
Collection of: Elizabeth Scofield

5.3 *Date Made: First quarter of the 20th century*
Description: A linen tea cloth with embroidery and cutwork. The cloth has four identical scenes on the filet lace border. Each scene has six figures. This cloth is excellent quality. Pieces of this quality are difficult to locate in today's market.
Measurements: Overall dimensions: 32" square
Collection of: Elizabeth Scofield

5.4 *Detail*

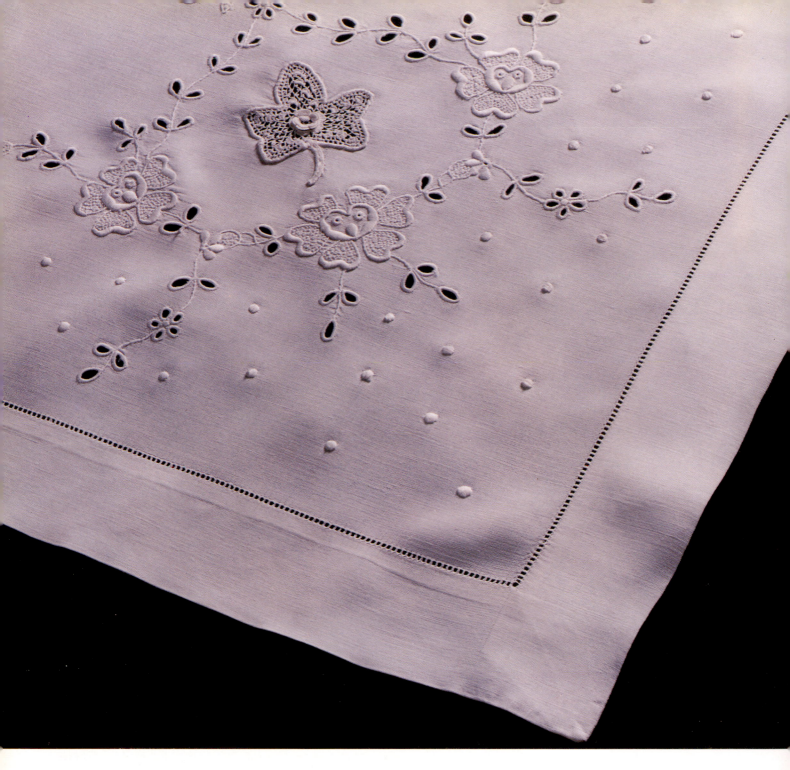

5.5 Origin: *Ireland*

Date Made: *First quarter of the 20th century*

Description: *A linen, eyelet tea cloth with a cluster of flowers and a three leaf clover in each corner. Each three leaf clover has an Irish crocheted insertion with a rose in the center. This tablecloth is unusual because Irish crochet is not usually used as an insertion.*

Measurements: *Overall dimensions: 34" square*

Collection of: *Helen Skelton*

5.6 Origin: *Italy*

Place Made: *First quarter of the 20th century*

Description: *Large, round, linen, figural lace tablecloth. An excellent example of combination lace household linen made in Italy in the early 20th century. The piece has four small figural and four large figural needle lace insertions. In addition it has four small non-figural and four large figural filet lace insertions. The border is filet lace. There is extensive cutwork, eyelet and satin stitch embroidery on the linen ground. The embroidery is average quality; however, the workmanship in the remainder of the piece is excellent. Uneven quality is quite typical in large pieces where several people were involved in making different parts of the piece. Large round tablecloths, in general, are difficult to find. This, coupled with the numerous, large figural lace insertions makes this piece very desirable. This piece has a faint nickel-sized inkspot.*

Measurements: *Diameter: 90"*

Dimensions of filet lace in photograph 5.8: 12.5"L x 11"W

Dimensions of needle lace insertion in photograph 5.7: 12"L x 11"W

Collection of: *Peggy Zalamea*

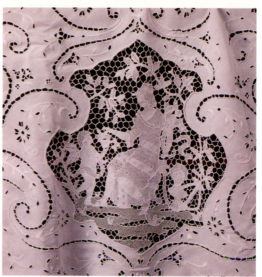

5.7 *Detail of a needle lace insertion from the tablecloth.*

5.8 *Detail of a filet lace insertion from the tablecloth featured in photograph 5.6.*

5.9 Origin: Madeira
Date Made: 1910-1930
Description: A linen table runner with cutwork, machine-made needle lace insertions, and a filet lace border which is machine-made. There are six insertions in the runner. They are surrounded by cutwork and embroidery. This type of runner was a very popular household item from 1910 to 1930. It is collectible only when it is in excellent condition.
Measurements: Overall dimensions: 18"L x 51.5"W
Collection of: Elizabeth Scofield

5.10 Date Made: *First quarter of the 20th century*
Description: Seven pieces of common household linen from the first
quarter of the 20th century. Pictured from the top left to the bottom are:
A pillowcase with cutwork and three filet lace insertions, four needle
lace insertions, and a filet lace border. A round figural doily with a filet
lace insertion and border. A child's cotton pillowcase with cutwork
embroidery and machine-made needle lace insertions. Two embroi-
dered square doilies with filet lace insertions and a filet lace border. An
oval embroidered doily with cutwork and filet lace insertions and
border. A linen hand towel with cutwork embroidery, a filet lace
insertion, and a filet lace border on the top and bottom.
All these pieces are good quality and are collectible. The pillowcase,
towel, and round doily are not as easy to find as the other four pieces.

Measurements: Overall dimensions of pillowcase: 32"L x 21.5"W
Diameter of round doily: 11"
Overall dimensions of the child's pillowcase: 12"L x 16"W
Dimensions of large square doily: 11.25" square
Dimensions of small square doily: 6.25" square
Dimensions of oval doily: 6"L x 9"W
Dimensions of hand towel: 22"L x 14"W
Pillowcase, collection of: Anna Burns
Round doily, collection of: Peggy Zalamea
Child's pillowcase, collection of: Elizabeth Scofield
Square doilies, collection of: Anna Burns
Oval doily, collection of: Elizabeth Scofield
Hand towel, collection of: Anna Burns

5.11 *Origin: Italy*
Date Made: Second quarter of the 20th century
Description: A cutwork linen placemat with needle lace insertions and
a figural filet lace border. This is an unusual combination of lace in a
placemat. Filet lace borders on placemats are usually less than one inch
in width with a floral design. This placemat has a figural filet lace
border that is three and one half to five inches in depth. This is a
collectible piece at an affordable price.
Measurements: Overall dimensions: 19"L x 13"W
Collection of: Peggy Zalamea

5.12 *Date Made: Early 20th century*
Description: A linen napkin with a figural needle lace insertion and a filet lace border. This is from a set of twelve napkins in excellent condition. Napkins in sets this size are difficult to find.
Measurements: Overall dimensions: 24" square
Collection of: Elizabeth Scofield

5.13 *Origin: Italy*
Date Made: First quarter of the 20th century
Description: An eyelet linen runner with figural, filet lace insertions and border, together with a linen, cutwork dinner napkin with a filet lace insertion and border. The runner is a very interesting piece for a number of reasons. The filet lace border on the runner has four different kinds of animals. Although we have also seen this type of figural border on small round tablecloths, a floral filet lace border is more typical for pieces from this period. The main filet lace panel in the runner is also unusual because it is made with two different types of thread to create some contrast in the figures. This is a less common type
of filet lace insertion than the four smaller squares in this same piece. This runner is difficult to find and is highly collectible. The napkin is one of a set of twelve. Sets of this quality are in demand and should sell for considerably more than a comparable size set of linen damask napkins. Some of the napkins in this set still have the original Made in Italy store labels sewn on them.
Measurements: Overall dimensions of runner: 18"L x 51"W
Dimensions of center filet lace insertion: 7"L x 19"W
Overall dimensions of napkin: 22" square
Collection of: Peggy Zalamea

5.16 Origin: *U.S.A.*

Date Made: *Turn of the century*

Description: *This linen cutwork bed cover has cotton filet lace and linen bobbin lace insertions as well as a bobbin lace border. Although the overall design is quite pleasing, the linen is rather coarse and the bobbin lace is of average quality. This type of bed cover can still be purchased at a relatively low price in today's market.*

Measurements: *Overall dimensions: 86"L x 82"W*

Collection of: *Peggy Zalamea*

5.17 *Origin: England*
Date Made: Turn of the century
Description: This embroidered, linen bed cover has linen bobbin lace
insertions as well as a bobbin lace border. It has nineteen embroidered
floral panels. Each one is slightly different in design. The linen is very
heavy which is typical for English bed linen of this period. The embroi-
dery is very good and the overall quality of this piece is several steps
above the bed cover in photograph 5.16.
Measurements: Overall dimensions: 102"L x 71"W
Collection of: Peggy Zalamea

5.18 Origin: Italy

Date Made: First quarter of the 20th century

Description: This cutwork linen bed cover has twenty-nine figural filet lace insertions of varying sizes, three figural cutwork panels, bobbin lace insertions, and a bobbin lace border.   The filet lace figures are very typical of the period; however, the cutwork figures are quite bizarre and everyone we have shown this piece to has a different opinion of what the figures are. We have seen at least one other bed cover with an identical design. However, the themes in the figural insertions were different. This piece is highly collectible.

Measurements: Overall dimensions: 89"L x 73"W

Dimensions of cutwork panels: 6"L x 6.5"W

Dimensions of largest filet lace panels: 8.5"L x 9"W

Collection of: Peggy Zalamea

5.19 Detail of one of the three cutwork panels.

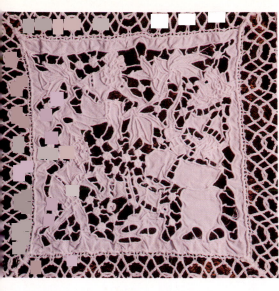

5.20 *Detail of one of the three cutwork panels.*

5.21 *Detail of one of the three cutwork panels.*

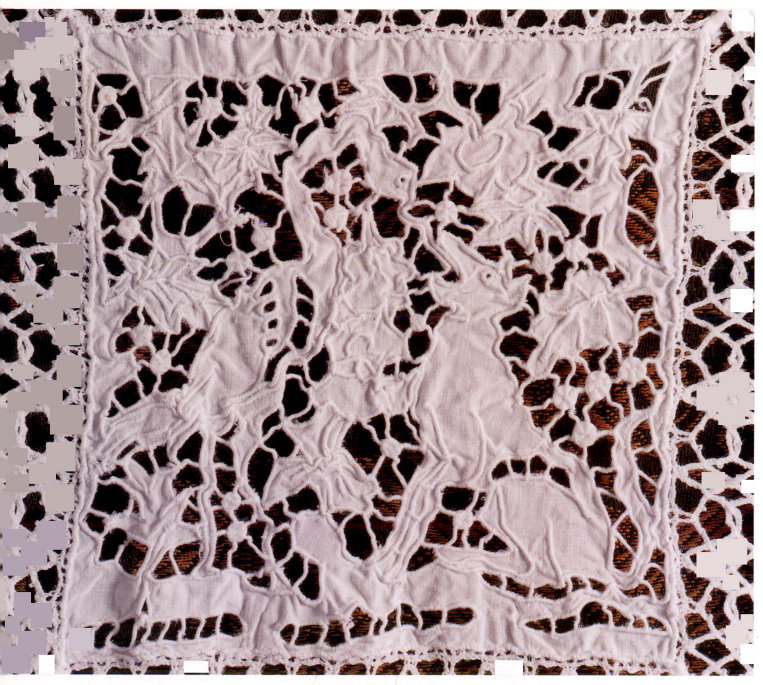

5.22 *Date Made: First quarter of the 20th century*

Description: This interesting peach and ivory linen bed cover contains embroidery, drawnwork, bobbin lace and figural needle lace. Forty-three needle lace figures stand in the doorways of palaces made out of embroidery and drawnwork. Bobbin lace insertions and drawnwork form a centerpiece around which the figures are grouped. There is a lace tassel, one of which is missing on each corner. The main part of the background consists of peach colored linen; however, the left and right sides end in a 10.5 inch ivory linen strip. There are two small repairs to the peach linen on the upper right corner as well as some fading in the peach linen at the top. The condition is good and workmanship is excellent. This piece is very collectible.

Measurements: Overall dimensions: 100"L x 90"W
Dimensions of the largest embroidered palaces: 7"L x 1.5"W
Dimensions of the largest needle lace people: 2"L x 1.5"W
Length of bobbin lace tassels: 3.5"
Collection of: Peggy Zalamea

5.23 *Overview of bed cover pictured in photograph 5.22.*

5.24 Date Made: Turn of the century
Description: This is one of a pair of curtains with bobbin lace and filet lace insertions. The two types of square, figural, filet lace insertions make this piece unusual. A more typical configuration of lace, wherein there is a continuous run of non-figural lace all along the borders of a machine net panel, can be seen in the example of curtains in Chapter Two. The length of each panel, the excellent condition, and the atypical layout of the figural lace make this piece very collectible.
Measurements: Overall dimensions of each panel: 128"L x 37"W
Dimensions of figural filet lace insertions: 9.5"L x 8.5"W
Collection of: Peggy Zalamea

5.25 Date Made: First quarter of the 20th century
Description: Square linen tea cloth with a wide bobbin lace border and needle lace inserts. This piece is excellent quality.
Measurements: Overall Dimensions: 30" square
Width of border: Varies from 3.5" to 8.5"
Dimensions of needle lace insertions 1.25"L x 1.25"W
Collection of: Elizabeth Scofield

5.26 *Origin: France*
Date Made: First half of the 20th century
Description: A French dresser scarf and a cushion cover showing two types of machine lace-bobbin and tape. The dresser scarf and the cushion cover have lovely patterns of flowers applied to the machine-made net, and machine-made tape lace borders that are hand applied.
Measurements: Overall dimensions of dresser scarf: 34" L x 16"W
Overall dimensions of cushion cover: 20.5"L x 15.5"W
Dresser scarf, collection of: Elizabeth Scofield
Cushion cover, collection of: Peggy Zalamea

5.27 *Date Made: First quarter of the 20th century*

Description: This is an excellent example of a cutwork and embroidered tablecloth with figural filet lace insertions, and a filet lace border. Four of the figural insertions are of a bird, four are of a single cherub, four depict two cherubs dancing, and two depict three cherubs in a scene. This type of tablecloth is very collectible because of the subject matter, cherubs and birds, and because of the extensive amount of cutwork and embroidery it has. The border has alternating flowers and leaves.

Measurements: Overall dimensions: 102"L x 72.5"W

Dimensions of largest insertion: 10"L x 9"W

Collection of: Mrs. Gertrude Hermann

5.29 Detail of photograph 5.27.

5.28 Detail of photograph 5.27.

5.30 Detail of photograph 5.27.

6.2 *Origin: U.S.A.*

Date Made: First half of the 20th century

Description: A figural crocheted tray cover; a linen damask hand towel with a crocheted insert; a crocheted bread doily and a crocheted glass coaster. The bread doily and the coaster are very common pieces. The crocheted initial on the hand towel is also very typical and was often done on bed sheets and pillowcases as well. The tray cover depicting the three deer, is not as easy to find. It is a nice piece to have in a collection of crochet and has the best chance of appreciating in value. All four pieces are very inexpensive.

Measurements: Overall dimensions of doily: "8L x "4W

Diameter of coaster: 5"

Overall dimensions of hand towel: 27.25"L x 14.25"W

Overall dimensions of tray cover: 18"L x 34"W

6.3 *Origin: U.S.A.*

Date Made: First quarter of the 20th century

Description: A figural crocheted tray cover. Butterflies are a common theme in crochet. Pieces like these are not difficult to find.

Measurements: Overall dimensions: 16"L x 18"W

Collection of: Peggy Zalamea

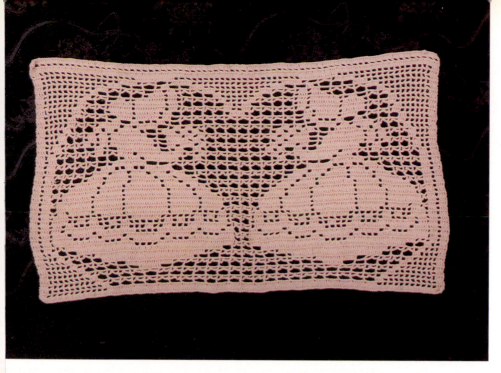

6.4 *Origin: U.S.A.*
Date Made: First quarter of the 20th century
Description: A figural crocheted tray cover.
Measurements: Overall dimensions: 9"L x 16"W
Collection of: Peggy Zalamea

6.5 *Origin: U.S.A. or England*
Date Made: First quarter of the 20th century
Description: A linen tea cloth with a crocheted insertion of a teapot, creamer, and sugar bowl. This is a typical motif of that period and pieces like this are not difficult to find.
Measurements: Overall dimensions: 34.25"L x 35"W
Dimensions of crocheted insertion: 4.25"L x 12"W
Collection of: Peggy Zalamea

6.10 Origin: U.S.A.

Date Made: First Quarter of the 20th century

Description: One of a pair of crocheted cushions. The workmanship
and design are excellent. A very inexpensive, highly decorative piece.

Measurements: Overall dimensions: 15" square

Collection of: Peggy Zalamea

6.11 Origin: U.S.A.

Date Made: First quarter of the 20th century

Description: A filet crocheted throw with a figural design. The owner of
this piece calls it "Rebecca at the Well" after a scene in the Bible. The
design and workmanship are excellent. This is a very collectible piece.

Measurements: Overall dimensions excluding fringe: 46"L x 35"W

Width of fringe: 4.25"L

Collection of: Jane Stief

6.12 Origin: U.S.A.

Date Made: Turn of the century

Description: A figural filet crocheted single curtain panel. The owner of this piece calls it "Christopher Columbus". The design and workmanship are excellent. Figural crocheted curtain panels of this size are rare and this piece is very collectible.

Measurements: Overall dimensions excluding fringe: 83"L x   50"W

Width of fringe: 5"

Dimensions of figure: 44.5"H x 15"W

Collection of: Tracylee Guerin

6.16 *Origin: U.S.A.*

Date Made: First quarter of the 20th century

Description: A filet crocheted curtain with three tassels. This piece has a cherub with a bow and arrow in the center. There is a garland of flowers surrounding the cherub. The design makes this interesting and collectible.

Measurements: Overall dimensions: 12" square

Height of the cherub: 9.5"

Collection of: Elizabeth Scofield

6.17 *Origin: U.S.A.*

Date Made: Second quarter of the 20th century

Description: A round crocheted doily. The workmanship is very good. This type of doily is easy to find at flea markets and antique shows.

Measurements: Diameter: 15"

Collection of: Elizabeth Scofield

6.18 *Origin: U.S.A.*

Date Made: 1900-1945

Description: A crocheted antimacassar set; a filet crocheted pillow, and an Irish crocheted bed cover. The antimacassar set was made by Ada Ford, Newark, Delaware, in 1950. The set is very well made and it is collectible because it is complete. The pillow has the faces of Washington and Lincoln outlined on it. It is a collectible piece from the 1940s when there were intense patriotic feelings in the United States. The bed cover has three hundred crocheted sections with a rose in the center of each. It is a good example of Irish crochet.

Measurements: Overall dimensions of the headrest: 8"L x 18"W

Overall dimensions of the armrest: 10.5"L x 11"W

Overall dimensions of the pillow: 12.5"L x 16"W

Dimensions of the figures in the pillow: Washington: 11"L x 7" W

Lincoln: 9"L x 5"W

Overall dimensions of the bed cover: 92"L x 72"W

Antimacassar set, collection of: Ada Ford

Pillow, collection of: James C. Ford

Bed cover, collection of: Elizabeth Scofield

6.22 Origin: U.S.A.

Date Made: 1929

Description: A figural, filet lace crocheted bed cover and sham. The sham depicts two hunters, two dogs and an elk. The name of the family who owned the sham, Stephenson, the year it was made, 1929, and the words "Sweet Sleep" are included in the design. The bed cover depicts two elk grazing in a field with sixteen birds flying or perched above them. The edges of the sham and bed cover are scalloped. This piece is collectible because it is difficult to find large figural pieces, and it has an unusual design.

Measurements: Overall dimensions of the sham: 72"W x 24.5"L

Overall dimensions of the bed cover: 66"L x 72"W

Dimensions of the elk: 22"W x 14.5"H

Collection of: Elizabeth Scofield

6.23 *Origin: U.S.A.*
Date Made: Second half of the 20th century
Description: A common crocheted doily with the pineapple design.
Measurements: Diameter: 11.5"
Collection of: Elizabeth Scofield

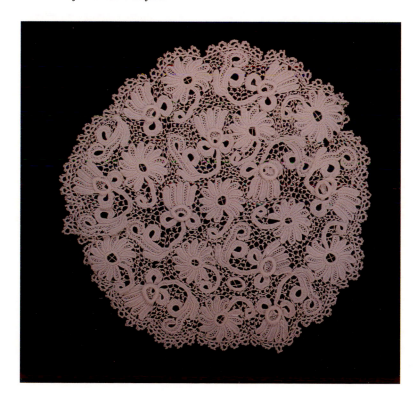

6.24 *Date Made: First quarter of the 20th century*
Description: An Irish crocheted doily that resembles needle lace. The doily consists of twenty-two flowers and ten densely packed rings. This piece is good quality.
Measurements: Diameter: 11"
Collection of: Elizabeth Scofield

Cutwork is one of the earliest forms of lace. It began in the 16th century and continues to be made in much the same fashion today. In cutwork, a pattern is traced onto the fabric and the design is outlined on the cloth with a basting stitch. These stitches are then covered with buttonhole stitches before parts of the underlying material are cut away to form open spaces, thereby creating a pattern. Afterwards, these open spaces are often filled in with lace inserts or with bars also covered with buttonhole stitches.

Cutwork is commonly done on linen or cotton and more recently on synthetic fabrics. It is rarely done on silk. The embroidery is usually done in the same color thread as the fabric although different colored thread can be used. Twentieth century cutwork pieces often appear to have been made with blue thread on white fabric. The thread is actually white, but the blue pencil or chalk that is used to trace the design onto the fabric shows through the white thread. The blue marks disappear after repeated washings. Older pieces that still have this bluish look probably have hardly been used.

Cutwork has been used to make all types of household linen. It continues to be made today all over the world. However, the bulk of new production is done in China on cotton fabric. With the exception of figural pieces, small, good quality 20th century cutwork is plentiful and relatively inexpensive. A good example of figural cutwork is pictured in photogaph 7.4. Linen cutwork, while also easy to find, is less common than cotton and usually commands higher prices.

7.1 Origin: Madeira (napkin) and Italy (tray cover)
Date Made: First half of the 20th century
Description: An oval figural cutwork linen tray cover and a cutwork linen dinner napkin (part of a set of four). Rectangular tray covers are more common than oval ones. This, coupled with the fact that this piece is figural, makes it a nice addition to any collection. The napkin is very common and inexpensive.
Measurements: Overall dimensions of tray cover: 16"L x 32.5"W
Dimensions of figure: 2.5"H x 1.25"W
Overall dimensions of napkin: 16" square
Collection of: Peggy Zalamea

7.3 *Date Made: First quarter of the 20th century*
Description: A single figural cutwork cotton curtain panel with crocheted border. Figural cutwork curtain panels are rare and highly collectible.
Measurements: Overall dimensions: 51"L x 18.5"W
Dimensions of figure: 4"H x 3.5"W
Collection of: Peggy Zalamea

7.2 *Date Made: First half of the 20th century*
Description: A cutwork linen tea cloth. The corner diagonally opposite the corner in the picture has an identical flower basket. The two other corners have smaller, similar, cutwork flower baskets. The beribboned flower basket is another common theme in 20th century household linen. This is a pretty, inexpensive tea cloth with good workmanship.
Measurements: Overall dimensions: 40"square
Dimensions of flower basket: 11.5"H x 14"W
Collection of: Peggy Zalamea

7.4 *Date Made: First quarter of the 20th century*
Description: A beautiful cotton cutwork panel. The panel has a large oval medallion near the bottom with two maidens sitting under a tree and two rows of cutwork with leaves and grapes going down each side. Three sides of the panel have scalloped embroidered edges.
Measurements: Overall dimensions: 73"L x 57"W
Dimensions of medallion: 19"L x 24.5"W
Height of the maidens: 8"
Collection of: Marci Lotman

7.5 *Date Made: First half of the 20th century*
Description: A cutwork sheet with matching pillowcases.
The sheet has two cutwork bows on either side of the top, with a large
medallion of cutwork centered between them. This set is average
quality. It is collectible because it is a set.
Measurements: Overall dimensions of the sheet: 95"L x 88"W
Dimensions of the large medallion in the sheet: 7"L x 13.5W
Overall dimensions of the pillowcase: 33"L x 21.5"W
Dimensions of the medallion in the pillowcases: 4"L x 7.5"W
Collection of: Elizabeth Scofield

7.6 *Date Made:* *First quarter of the 20th century*
Description: *Two wonderful cutwork cats in a hand-painted wooden frame. The cats are separated by a butterfly. The piece is in excellent condition. This piece is collectible because of its subject matter.*
Measurements: *Overall dimensions: 17"L x 19"W*
Dimensions of the cats: 6"L x 3"W
Collection of: *Elizabeth Scofield*

7.7 *Origin:* *Italy*
Date Made: *Turn of the century*
Description: *A figural, cutwork, linen cushion cover with a filet lace border. Rare and highly desirable.*
Measurements: *Overall dimensions: 13"L x 16.5"W*
Dimensions of figure: 4.5"H x 3.75"W
Collection of: *Peggy Zalamea*

7.8 Origin: *Madeira, Portugal*
Date Made: *First half of the 20th century*
Description: *A cutwork cotton tablecloth with twelve napkins. (The napkins are not shown.) A wonderful example of cutwork. Note how the design covers almost every inch of fabric. There is a frayed area the size of a dime, which is almost impossible to notice. We consider this tablecloth to be in good condition, hard to find, and quite collectible.*
Measurements: *Overall dimensions: 99"L x 67"W*
Collection of: *Peggy Zalamea*

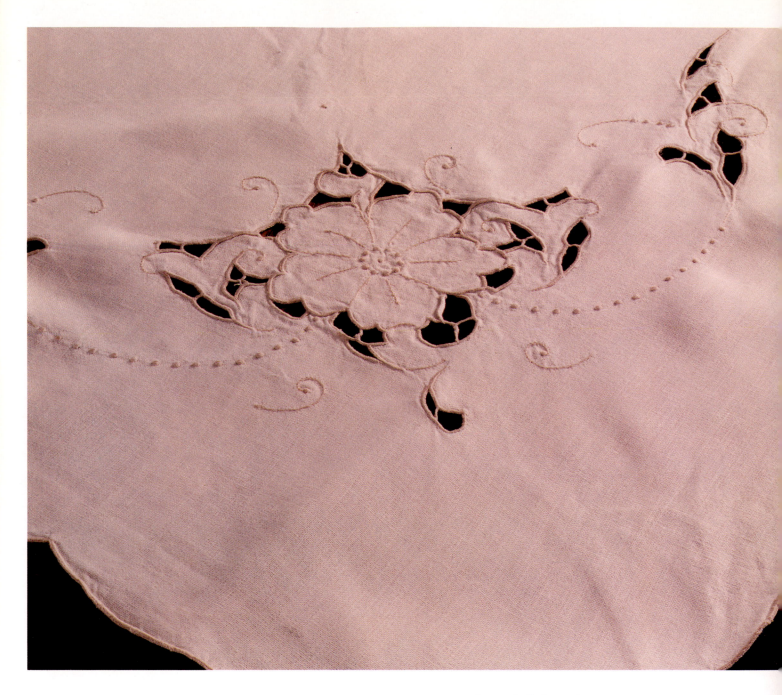

7.10 Origin: *Madeira, Portugal*
Date Made: *Second half of the 20th century*
Description: *A cutwork linen tablecloth made in Madeira. This is a
poor example of Madeira work. The cutwork is not very extensive, and
the design is uninteresting. Note that the open spaces are outlined with
brown thread which contrasts with the cream colored fabric. This is very
typical of Madeira work. The best examples of Madeira work are worth
collecting; however, examples such as this one will probably not
appreciate in value very quickly. This type of tablecloth is readily
available.*
Measurements: *Overall dimensions: 113"L x 58"W*
Collection of: *Peggy Zalamea*

7.11 Date Made: *First half of the 20th century*
Description: *A cotton cutwork runner, a figural cotton cutwork napkin,
a linen cutwork napkin, and a cotton cutwork placemat. Each napkin
is part of a set of eight. The cotton napkin with a stag in one corner is
the most interesting piece in this photograph. This napkin is the most
collectible piece because cutwork figural napkins are difficult to find.
The workmanship in the first three pieces is average while the workman-
ship in the placemat is very poor. The thread around the cut edges is so
sparse that the raw edges are partially visible. This placemat is a typical
example of the lower end items being made in Madeira.*
Measurements: *Overall dimensions of the runner: 41"L x 16"W*
Overall dimensions of figural napkin: 20" square
Overall dimensions of linen napkin: 16" square
Overall dimensions of placemat: 15.5"L x 10"W
Runner and linen napkin, collection of: Peggy Zalamea
Figural napkin, collection of: Anna Burns
Placemat, collection of: Elizabeth Scofield

8.2 *Origin: Maderia, Portugal*
Date Made: Second quarter of the 20th century
Description: An organdy placemat with a linen appliquéd border and a
linen napkin with an organdy insertion. Each placemat and napkin
has an appliquéd fish gracefully swimming on it. The placemat and
napkin are part of a set of eight. The set is unusual, and it is difficult to
find sets of eight or more placemats with matching napkins.
Measurements: Overall dimensions of placemat: 18.5"W x 12"L
Overall dimensions of napkin: 16.75"L x 16.75"W
Collection of: Anna Burns

8.3 *Date Made: First quarter of the 20th century*
Description: Five pieces of eyelet linen. These pieces were common
household linen in the first quarter of the 20th century. The round
tablecloth is unusual because it has eight large and four small embroi-
dered birds on it. The cotton pillowcase has floral embroidery and
eyelet around the border. The child's pillowcase has a scalloped
embroidered edge with a row of eyelet going around it. The coaster is a
standard pattern. The oval doily is very well done with beautiful
embroidery. The most collectible piece in the ensemble is the tablecloth
because it is figural.

Measurements: Diameter of tablecloth: 68"
Overall dimensions of child's pillowcase: 13"L x 17"W
Overall dimensions of pillowcase: 32"L x 30"W
Overall dimensions of doily: 10.5"L x 5.5"W
Diameter of coaster: 6"
Tablecloth, collection of: Elizabeth Scofield
Pillowcase, collection of: Kay Mertens
Child's pillowcase, collection of: Elizabeth Scofield
Oval doily, collection of: Elizabeth Scofield
Coaster, collection of: Peggy Zalamea

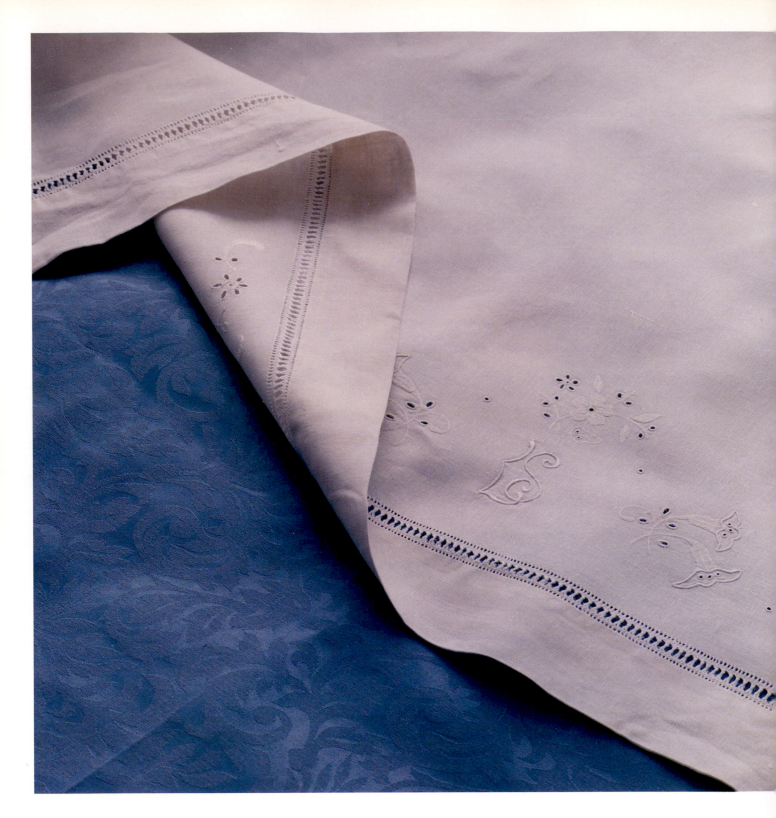

8.4 *Origin: Italy*
Date Made: First quarter of the 20th century
*Description: A linen bed sheet with eyelet and shadow stitch embroidery
and drawnwork. Large old linen bed sheets are highly desirable and
still affordable. Most early 20th century bed linen was monogrammed
so the monogram should not affect the value.*
Measurements: Overall dimensions: 98"L x 92"W
Collection of: Peggy Zalamea

8.5 Origin: *Madeira*

Date Made: *First quarter of the 20th century*

Description: *A cotton cutwork and embroidered bed sheet with a matching pair of pillowcases. The gray pencil used to trace the design on the cotton is still apparent which probably means that this set was not used very much. The underlying marks disappear only after repeated washing. The cotton is still quite stiff which also points to infrequent use. The theme of birds in a bird bath is desirable and the workmanship is excellent. The value is also enhanced because this is a complete set.*

Measurements: *Overall dimensions of bed sheet: 100"L x 88"W*
Overall dimensions of the pillowcases: 33.5"L x 20.5"W

Collection of: *Peggy Zalamea*

8.6 Origin: Italy
Date Made: First quarter of the 20th century
Description: An embroidered cotton bed sheet with drawnwork together with a similar sham. These two pieces were made as part of trousseau sets. The family name was often part of the embroidered design. As an alternative, greetings such as good night or good morning were often incorporated into the embroidery. The bed sheets were usually made to fit a queen size bed. Individual bed sheets and shams are easy to find and quite inexpensive. Complete sets consisting of a bed sheet with two matching shams are harder to find and more expensive.
Measurements: Overall dimensions of bedsheet: 114" L x 96"
Overall dimensions of sham: 31"L x 39"W
Collection of: Peggy Zalamea

8.7 Date Made: First quarter of the 20th century
Description: An embroidered linen bed cover with drawnwork. This is one of a pair, easy to find, and inexpensive.
Measurements: Overall dimensions: 107"L x 70"W
Collection of: Peggy Zalamea

8.10 Origin: *U.S.A.*

Date Made: *First quarter of the 20th century*

Description: *A linen drawnwork tea cloth embroidered with colored silk thread. This kind of embroidery was done in the U.S. throughout the first half of the 20th century. The embroidery was usually floral in design. This piece is one of the finer examples of this type of work that we have seen. Still relatively easy to find but prices are rising.*

Measurements: *Overall dimensions: 38"L x 36"W*

Collection of: *Kay Mertens*

8.11 Date Made: *First quarter of the 20th century*
Description: *A figural, eyelet linen tablecloth with a scalloped, embroidered border. The cloth has four lovely baskets of flowers centered on each of its edges and numerous other patterns. The workmanship is very good and the basket theme enhances its collectibility.*
Measurements: *Overall dimensions: 83.5"L x 66"W*
Dimensions of the basket: *10.5"L x 6"W*
Collection of: *Elizabeth Scofield*

8.12 *Detail of flower basket in tablecloth.*

9.2 Origin: *Madeira*
Date Made: *Mid 20th century*
Description: *Eight embroidered cocktail napkins in their original box.*
The label reads "Paragon Needlecraft, hand embroidery, Madeira".
Measurements: *Overall dimension of each napkin: 3.5L x 6.5W*
Height of the largest figure: *3.5"*
Collection of: *Dr. Leonard G. Scofield*

9.3 *Date Made: 1940-1960*
Description: Two appliqué and embroidered napkins from a set of eight. The napkins have an embroidered scalloped edge. These napkins were used for fun at cocktail parties.
Measurements: Overall dimensions: 5"L x 6.5"W
Height of figures: 4"
Collection of: Dr. Leonard G. Scofield

9.4 *Origin: Madeira, Portugal*
Date Made: Second quarter of the 20th century
Description: An organdy cocktail napkin with linen appliqué. This napkin is one of a set of eight. Napkins with rooster motifs were quite popular during this period.
Measurements: Overall dimensions: 5.25"L x 7.75"W
Collection of: Anna Burns

9.5 *Date Made: 1950-1960*
Description: Three cocktail napkins and ten coasters. The napkins have a rooster embroidered on one corner and a scalloped embroidered border. The ten coasters have scalloped embroidered edges and there is a rooster embroidered on each of them.
Measurements: Overall dimensions of the napkins: 5.5" square
Diameter of the coasters: 3"
Collection of: Elizabeth Scofield

Using Jennifer Harris' definition from *Textiles–Five Thousand Years*, damask is a textile that "combines warp-faced and weft-faced twill or satin sections and is always reversible, because a pattern area with warp floats on one side will have equal weft floats on the other."

Traditional damask has always been white-on-white. Prior to the 19th century, damask was the only linen fabric used in the dining rooms of the elite. Damask became more affordable in the 19th century with the use of the Jacquard loom coupled with the increasing substitution of cotton for linen or silk which are more expensive fabrics. By the 1920s, even women with slim purses could manage to save their pennies to acquire one perfect set of damask linen for formal entertaining. Damask has become even more affordable in the latter parts of this century due to the advent of synthetic fibers.

Although colored damask first appeared in the 19th century, it was not accepted for use as table linen until after the first World War. Even then, colored damask was considered a very informal look more suitable for luncheon table settings as opposed to dinner settings where only white-on-white linen was acceptable. Colored damask gave women an opportunity to vary their table settings with a tablecloth, crystal, china, and floral arrangements each in a different pastel shade, blending together harmoniously.

Figural damask linen made prior to the 20th century is very valuable. Francoise de Bonneville in *The Book of Fine Linen* mentions that a single napkin depicting the battle of Fontenoy currently costs approximately 80,000 French francs (US$ 15,203.00).

In general, flowers have been the most common theme in 20th century damask. The tablecloth pictured in photograph 10.3 is a typical example. During a brief period in the 1920s and 1930s, multi-colored, geometric Art Deco designs were in vogue. Two examples of Art Deco designs in damask are pictured in photograph 10.2. It should be noted that some figural themes have also been used in the 20th century, but they are not common. A rare set of 20th century figural linen damask napkins is pictured in photograph 10.1.

The quality of 20th century linen damask varies widely from piece to piece. Many tablecloths and napkins are very rough with indistinct patterns. In the finest damask, the fabric is smooth to the touch and the satin sections that form the pattern stand out clearly.

In these days of disposable napkins and plastic placemats, damask table linen is no longer used in everyday living. However, there is still nothing to compare with a dining table set with fine linen to bring a touch of elegance to formal occasions.

Large early 20th century dinner napkins in sets of six or more are always sought after, particularly in areas like Philadelphia and New York. Sets of twelve or more dinner napkins are becoming difficult to find. Tablecloths seating six to eight people are readily available. However, tablecloths seating twelve or more people are rare and very expensive. Plain linen damask placemats and runners are relatively rare but do not appear to be in great demand. More ornate placemats and runners trimmed with lace or decorated with cutwork or embroidery are much more desirable and, consequently, more expensive. Colored damask table linens are currently highly sought after and often sell for more than comparable quality white damask pieces.

Today, the finest damasks are produced in Ireland, Italy, and France. Linen, cotton, and synthetic fibers are used in damask made for all kinds of household use. Silk damask is more commonly used for upholstery material and bed covers.

10.1 Origin: Ireland
Date Made: First quarter of the 20th century
Description: A double damask dinner napkin with the original store label. The "Shakespeare" pattern is woven into one edge. The napkin is one of a set of twenty-four napkins. This set is rare because it is figural and part of an extremely large set. Please note that this napkin has been improperly stored in a folded position for so long that the fold lines could not be removed by ironing them.
Measurements: Overall dimensions: 22"square
Collection of: Peggy Zalamea

10.2 *Date Made: First half of the 20th century*
Description: A figural napkin, two Art Deco hand towels in lavender and yellow respectively, a blue and white towel, and a figural pink and white towel. The figural napkin is very pretty and is collectible because of the subject matter. Towels with an Art Deco theme are hard to find and are also collectible. The fact that they are not white also enhances their value. The blue and white towel reads "Panama-Pacific Expositions" and is dated 1915 in one corner. It is typical of linen damask made for hotels, restaurants, and other businesses catering to tourists and other travelers. This linen often has the company name or logo woven into the overall design. The pink and white towel has eleven birds woven in the pink band. The quality is not as good as that of the Art Deco towels but the subject matter makes it interesting.
Measurements: Overall dimensions of the napkin: 14"L x 13.75"W
Overall dimensions of the art deco towel: 34"L x 18"W
Overall dimensions of blue and white towel: 35.5"L x 28"W
Overall dimensions of pink and white towel: 29"L x 17"W
Napkin, collection of: Kay Mertens
Art deco towels, collection of: Peggy Zalamea
Two other towels, collection of: Richard King

10.3 *Origin: Ireland*
Date Made: First half of the 20th century
Description: Good quality medium size white linen damask tablecloth with a floral pattern. Easy to find and very affordable. Linen damask tablecloths of good or excellent quality that are at least one hundred forty inches long are harder to find and cost at least fifty percent more than the tablecloth shown here. This piece falls in the category of very useful but not very collectible linen. Colored damask tablecloths are becoming more popular and are harder to find.
Measurements: Overall dimensions: 88"L x 66"W
Collection of: Peggy Zalamea

10.4 *Date Made: First half of the 20th century*
Description: A yellow and white figural linen damask tablecloth with
drawnwork. The drawnwork outlining the cherub theme on the border
adds extra interest. Quite collectible.
Measurements: Overall dimensions: 58"L x 55"W
Collection of: Richard King

10.5 *Description: A floral yellow damask napkin and a yellow and white linen damask napkin. The pattern shown on the yellow napkin is* repeated in each corner. *Both napkins are good quality and both are easy to find.*
Measurements: 17" square
Yellow and white: 14" square

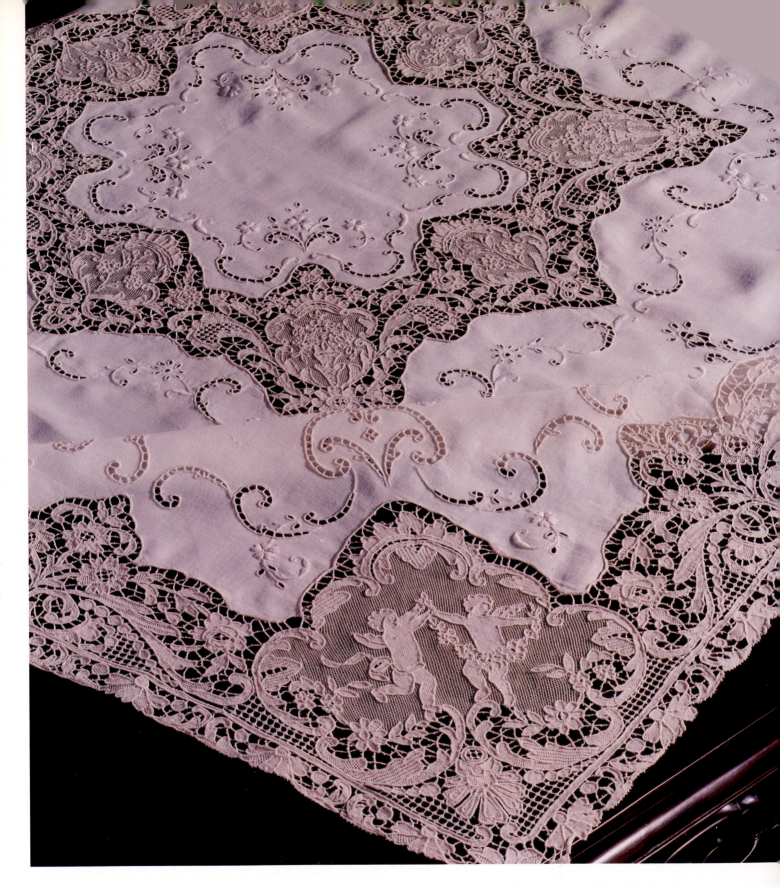

11.1 Origin: Italy

Date Made: Second quarter of the 20th century

Description: A linen cutwork tea cloth with an extensive number of needle lace inserts and a figural needle lace border. This is a wonderful piece with excellent workmanship. The two cherubs shown in this photograph are repeated in each corner. Peggy purchased this piece at an auction in Toronto in 1993. The catalogue described this piece as a tape lace tablecloth with an estimate of $60 to $90. This piece is rare and highly collectible.

Measurements: Overall dimensions: 50"L x 46"W

Dimensions of corner medallions: 11"H x 9.50"W

Height of cherubs: 3.75"

Collection of: Sue Zalamea

Needle lace is a derivation of embroidery. It began in the 16th century in France, Spain, and Venice. Needle lace is made with an ordinary sewing needle and single thread and is regarded as the finest of laces.

In its earliest form, needle lace was made in a fashion similar to cutwork embroidery and was called *Reticella*. Lacemakers would draw threads from pieces of woven fabric until only a few threads remained, then work designs into the open areas.

By the mid-16th century, needleworkers discovered that needle lace could be designed on a foundation of parchment or vellum by basting a framework of threads to either and filling the framework in with a series of fine buttonhole or decorative stitches on the surface of the vellum. This new technique lent itself to great freedom in design and was called *punto in aria* - stitches in air.

In the early 20th century there was a renewed interest in needle lace which was then being produced in China, Cyprus, and Italy. The most collectible pieces of household linen from this time period are figural examples from Italy.

There is a beautiful example of a figural needle lace tablecloth pictured in photograph 11.7. On a recent trip to Italy, Peggy saw an earlier example of comparable quality with a price tag of roughly $100,000! She was told that the shop where she saw this tablecloth charged five times the market price for linens and lace. Even allowing for this type of gross overpricing, $100,000 divided by five is still an incredible $20,000!

Needle lace is still being produced in Europe and Asia. The handmade pieces being produced today are made with rigid cotton thread and typically lack creativity in design.

We highly recommend that examples of figural needle lace be added to your collection. Both European and Chinese examples are considered collectible. However, European examples command much higher prices.

11.2 *Origin: Italy*
Date Made: Turn of the century
Description: A single curtain panel with needle lace border depicting two knights jousting with four squires in the background. The silk blend fabric was added later. Missing tassels do not affect the value of this piece. Neither does a quarter sized hole in the fabric at the top of the curtain. This is a great piece of needle lace and it is highly collectible.
Measurements: Overall dimensions: 85"L x 100"W
Dimensions of jousting knights: 7"H x 9.5"W
Collection of: Peggy Zalamea

11.3 *Origin: Italy*
Date Made: First quarter of the 20th century
*Description: An excellent quality needle lace cushion
cover with a linen back and a machine net ruffled
border.*
Measurements: Overall dimensions: 13"L x 16"W
Collection of: Peggy Zalamea

11.4 *Origin: Italy*
Date Made: First quarter of the 20th century
*Description: A linen tablecloth made in four sections
and joined by four strips of needle lace and a religious
needle lace insertion. Each of the four sections has a
needle lace insertion of a bird. The cloth is bordered in
linen needle lace.*
Measurements: Overall dimensions: 28"L x 40"W
Diameter of bird insertions: 3.25"
Dimensions of the religious insertion: 8"L x 4"W
Width of border: 4"
Collection of: Elizabeth Scofield

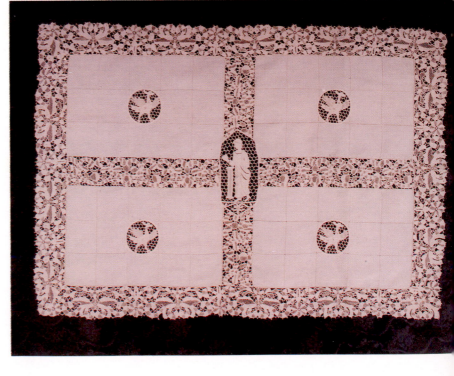

11.5 *Detail of photograph 11.4.*

11.6 *Detail of photograph 11.4.*

11.9 *Detail of photograph 11.7.*

11.10 *Detail of photograph 11.7.*

11.13 *Origin: Italy*

Date Made: Second quarter of the 20th century

Description: There are forty dancing girls and cherubs in this needle lace tablecloth. A much heavier cotton thread was used in this piece compared to that used in the tablecloth pictured in photograph 11.7. The workmanship and overall design are excellent. Note how many different types of filling stitches have been used and how the brides vary from one area to the next. Figural point de venise *pieces of this size and quality are rare. Chinese copies should not be confused with pieces made in Italy. Chinese copies are not as well made and should sell for much less.*

Measurements: Overall dimensions: 139"L x 63"W

Dimensions of largest figure: 4"L x 2.5"W

Dimensions of smallest figure: 3.5"L x 1.75"W

Collection of: Peggy Zalamea

11.14 *Detail*

11.15 Origin: Italy

Date Made: Turn of the century

Description: A very fine figural needle lace border for an oval tablecloth. The current owner purchased this piece in this condition and we
do not know what the original center of the tablecloth looked like. The
border is in excellent condition. It has eight large medallions depicting
different scenes. Four medallions have mythological themes while the
other four show various animals such as a dog chasing a stag. This is a
very rare and highly collectible piece.

Measurements: Overall dimensions: 364"L x 22"W

Average size of medallions: 11.5"L x 15"W

Height of largest figure: 6.5"

Collection of: Kay Mertens

11.16 *Detail of photograph 11.15.*

11.17 *Detail of photograph 11.15.*

11.18 *Detail of photograph 11.15.*

11.21 Origin: Italy

Date Made: First quarter of the 20th century

Description: A three piece needle lace antimacassar set of excellent quality. Complete sets are hard to find and are not in great demand.

Measurements: Overall dimensions of headrest: 11"L x 18"W

Overall dimensions of armrest: 11"L x 6.5"W

Collection of: Peggy Zalamea

11.22 Origin: Venice, Italy

Date Made: Second quarter of the 20th century

Description: A figural needle lace doily with a cutwork cotton center. An amazing amount of work went into making such a small piece. There are six figures in this doily. It is highly collectible.

Measurements: Overall dimensions: 7" diameter

Tallest figure: 2.25"H x 1.5"W

Collection of: Peggy Zalamea

11.23 Origin of Placemat and Matching Napkin: Italy
Origin of Placemat: China
Date Made: Second quarter of the 20th century
Description: Two needle lace placemats, three napkins, and two coasters. The placemat at the top left is Italian needle lace and three matching napkins from a set of four are shown with it. This set is of better quality than the other placemat in this photograph which was made in China. Neither placemat was made with fine thread which is typical of needle lace made after the first quarter of the 20th century. Italian needle lace placemats of this quality are still made today. However, new placemats sell for considerably more than this one. The Chinese placemat has little acorns incorporated in the design. This is a typical theme in Chinese needle lace pieces of this period. This kind of lace was also used in tablecloths and runners made in China in this period. The Italian pieces are more desirable and more expensive. Sets of eight or more Italian needle lace placemats with or without matching napkins are hard to find. The needle lace coasters are part of a set of five. Sets of coasters are still relatively easy to find.
Measurements: Overall dimensions of Italian placemat: 17.5"L X 11"W
Overall dimensions of Italian napkin: 16.5" square
Overall dimensions of Chinese placemat: 15"L x 10"W
Overall dimensions of coasters: 4.25" Diameter
Collection of: Peggy Zalamea

11.24 *Origin: Italy*

Date Made: Turn of the century

Description: This cotton figural point de venise *bed cover is one of a pair. Except for a small cigarette burn on one bed cover, both pieces are in excellent condition. It is rare to find even one figural needle lace bed cover. Although the overall pattern is not as dense as that of the tablecloths shown in photographs 11.7 and 11.13, the workmanship is excellent. In addition, the figures are unusually large with the tallest figure being fourteen inches tall. Highly collectible.*

Measurements: Overall dimensions: 83"L x 76.5"W

Dimensions of woman: 14"H x 10.5"W

Dimensions of largest cherub: 14"H x 14.5"W

Collection of: Peggy Zalamea

11.25 Origin: China
Date Made: Second quarter of the 20th century
Description: A needle lace tablecloth made with cotton thread. The cloth is coarse and the design lacks creativity. This tablecloth was included in this book for the purpose of comparison.
Measurements: Overall dimensions: 80"L x 58"W
Collection of: Elizabeth Scofield

12.1 Date Made: First quarter of the 20th century

Description: A figural filet lace bed cover with a scalloped edge with a flower and leaf design. This piece has two cherubs sitting back to back in each corner and four cherubs dancing in a circle in the center. It is collectible because large figural filet pieces are difficult to find and the subject matter, cherubs, is very popular. This bed cover was a gift to Liz from Peggy, Christmas 1993.

Measurements: Overall Dimensions: 90"L x 80"W

Dimensions of the corner cherubs: 10.5"L x 5.5"W

Dimensions of the center cherubs: 13"L x 5"W

Collection of: Elizabeth Scofield

Filet lace and buratto are two of the oldest existing laces. They came into general use in Europe in the Middle Ages and have been made continuously since then. The making of filet lace was a favorite pastime of queens and court ladies in the 16th and 17th centuries. Filet lace has also been called *Filet Brode* and lacis. In addition, depending on whom you talk to, filet lace has been referred to as a needle lace or a type of embroidery. To avoid confusion, in this book we will refer to it only as filet lace, a form of needle lace.

Filet lace has been one of the most popular laces since Victorian times. Its rise in popularity was due in great measure to the fact that handmade nets could be purchased in shops starting in the late 19th century. Prior to this marketing innovation, the nets had to be handmade at home. Net darning and filet lace are some of the easiest of the needle laces to make which accounts for their continuing popularity.

Filet lace consists of a hand-knotted net background upon which a pattern is later embroidered using a darning stitch (either linen stitch or toile reprise stitch). Net darning refers to hand embroidery on machine-made net. It simulates filet lace but is less expensive. Machine-made background is easy to identify because it does not have knots on each corner of each square in the mesh. Although machine-made nets simulating filet lace grounds were first introduced in the early 19th century, these nets were not readily available until the early 20th century when net darning became very popular. Pauline Knight in her book *Filet Lace Patterns* states that "the *London Correspondent*, in April 1908, told of squares of netting which could be bought ready for darning; the frames needed were already bound with green ribbon. Books of designs were printed on coloured grounds, the figures finding most favor being men on horseback, griffins and other such quaint subjects. These would be used for cushion covers, tea cloths, chair and sofa backs" (p.20).

Buratto looks similar to filet lace because the patterns are created using a darning stitch identical to that used in filet lace. However, it differs in that it has a background that is woven instead of knotted. Buratto and filet lace are similar in price, although filet lace is more common.

Filet lace, net darning, and buratto are commonly used for insertions or borders. Small, ready-made filet lace insertions became available in the early 20th century (photograph 12.8). A large number of these were purchased to be incorporated into larger pieces at home. Filet lace borders are common on napkins, hand towels, pillowcases, runners, doilies, tablecloths, and placemats, and, more rarely, on

matching pillowcase and bed sheet sets. Filet lace borders on placemats are typically less than one inch deep. Figural filet borders with a depth of two or more inches on placemats are rare. A rare example of a placemat with a very wide figural lace border is shown in photograph 5.11.

Filet lace was also used to make entire placemats, runners, round and square tea cloths, large round and rectangular tablecloths, and bed covers. Both fine and coarse thread are used in the above pieces. Different threads, in terms of thickness and even color, can be used in different parts of the pattern in one piece. However, the background of a piece is always made of one type of thread only. Very thick thread was used to make borders or entire curtain panels. In earlier times, gold and silver thread were often used in filet lace and buratto. Linen, silk and cotton were commonly used in the early part of the 20th century. Currently, synthetic threads are often used. Items made out of the natural fibers are typically more valuable than those made out of synthetic threads.

A large quantity of filet lace was made in England, Italy, and North America in the first half of the 20th century. Although these areas still produce filet lace today, the bulk of new production is in China. According to Pauline Knight in her book *Filet Lace Patterns*, "around about the 1930s pieces such as tray cloths and runners made on a knotted net ground of cotton and worked with a thick thread were exported from China, their designs either variants of the vine pattern or else of a guipure type. Their attractive cheapness meant that only the discriminating who could afford it bought English made lacis" (p. 25). An example of Chinese filet lace made in the 1930s is pictured in photograph 12.11. As with all other lace, items made in Europe and North America are more collectible and more expensive than Chinese filet lace made in the same period.

Figural filet lace and buratto pieces are very collectible. A complete set of six or more figural filet lace placemats is very rare. The larger pieces are also becoming difficult to find. Wonderful single figural filet lace and buratto placemats and small tea cloths are still easy to locate at very affordable prices. Many of the smaller pieces are being framed, made into cushions, or incorporated into larger pieces. Early 20th century large, figural pieces are also in great demand and continue to appreciate in value. A good example is the cherub bed cover featured in photograph 12.1. Good examples of filet lace and buratto are great additions to any collection.

12.2 *Date Made: Turn of the century*
Description: A figural linen buratto runner. The figures make this
runner interesting and collectible.
Measurements: Overall dimensions: 15"L x 46"W
Size of griffins: 4.5" H x 6.25"W
Collection of: Peggy Zalamea

12.3 *Origin: Italy*
Date Made: Turn of the century
Description: A figural filet lace runner. The classical theme of this
runner is typical of figural filet lace pieces made in the late Victorian
and early 20th century periods. This runner is very collectible.
Measurements: Overall dimensions: 14.5"L x 52"W
Height of largest figure: 11.5"H
Collection of: Peggy Zalamea

12.4 Description: A figural filet lace tablecloth with forty-six scenes of fruit and twenty-eight cherubs identical to the ones shown in this photograph. The cherubs are separated by bowls of fruit. This cloth is in good condition and it is collectible because of the unusual combination of cherubs and fruit.

Measurements: Overall dimensions: 72"L x 52"W
Height of cherubs: 4"

12.5 Date Made: First quarter of the 20th century
Description: A square filet lace table cover depicting four scenes of kings and knights. This piece is very well executed. Pieces of this quality are a good addition for your collection.

Measurements: Overall dimensions: 26" square
Collection of: Elizabeth Scofield

12.6 *Date Made: First quarter of the 20th century*
Description: A filet lace tablecloth. Large filet lace pieces are difficult to
find in perfect condition. Nevertheless, they are not in great demand
and prices, particularly for non-figural items, remain moderate.
Measurements: Overall dimensions: 72"L x 102"W
Collection of: Peggy Zalamea

12.7 *Origin: England*

Date Made: First quarter of the 20th century

Description: A filet lace bed cover and portier with a filet lace border. The work that went into making this bed cover was amazing. The traditional mesh background was made first. Then thread was loosely woven through the mesh to create the grapes and the overall circular pattern. Finally, needle lace leaves were sewn on to complete the grape vine design. This is a very fine and unusual example of filet lace in excellent condition. Silk thread was used to make the filet lace border of the portier. The upper portion consists of a linen blend fabric with a

small, coarse bobbin lace medallion applied to it. There is a large tear in the fabric which is hidden by the bobbin lace medallion. There are also minor runs in various parts of the fabric. Since this piece is average quality, the fact that it is only in fair condition plays a larger role in its valuation. Condition would have less of an impact on the price of the bed cover in this same photograph.

Measurements: Overall dimensions of the bed cover: 90"L x 100"W.

Overall dimensions of the portier: 86"L x 45"W

Height of portier's filet lace border: 18"

Collection of: Peggy Zalamea

12.8 *Date Made: First quarter of the 20th century*
Description: Fourteen filet lace insertions of various sizes and shapes.
This type of insert was sold in stores at the turn of the century. The
butterfly insertions have a price tag on them which reads "H.K. & Co. 5
cents." The large panel of lace in this photograph was part of the
trousseau of Mrs. Meta Burmeister, Grandmother of Lloyd Russow. She
made this piece in 1903.
Measurements: Dimensions of the filet panel: 8.5'L x 20"W
Dimension of the largest insert: 6.75" square
Dimension of the smallest insert: 1.75" square
Fillet panel, collection of: Mr. and Mrs. Lloyd Russow
Butterfly insertions, collection of: Mr. and Mrs. Gerald Marvin
Remaining pieces, collection of: Anna Burns

 12.9 *Date Made: First quarter of the 20th century*
Description: One panel of an unusual pair of figural linen buratto
curtains. Each curtain has four figural panels. Curtains with filet lace
or bobbin lace insertions are more common than curtains with buratto
work. This pair is in excellent condition and is highly collectible.
Measurements: Overall Dimensions: 76.5"L x 36.25"W
Dimensions of large center medallion: 24"L x 11.25"W
Height of figures in center medallion: 21"
Height of largest figure in border: 6.25"
Collection of: Tracylee Guerin

12.11 *Origin of runner: China*
Date Made (Runner): c. 1930
Date Made: (Coasters): 20th century
Description: Chinese filet lace runner and four coasters. The runner was made with a very coarse cotton thread and was one of the first attempts by the Chinese to copy European filet lace. This type of lace was used to make curtains, tablecloths, placemats, runners and bed covers. The four filet lace coasters are from a set of eight. They are examples of

filet lace that is still being made in Europe, North America and China today. It is virtually impossible to tell where and when these coasters were made. They are made with a much finer cotton thread than the runner. These pieces are easy to find and we do not expect their prices to rise in the near future.
Measurements: Overall Dimensions of the runner: 38"L x 13.25"W
Diameter of coasters: 6"
Collection of: Peggy Zalamea

12.12 Origin: Italy
Date Made: First quarter of the 20th century
Description: A figural filet lace placemat made with very fine cotton thread. Cherubs are a common theme in figural filet lace. The workmanship in this piece is very good. It is difficult to find a complete set of figural filet lace placemats. This piece is very collectible.
Measurements: Overall dimensions: 15"L x 10.5"W
Collection of: Peggy Zalamea

12.13 Date Made: First half of the 20th century
Description: A linen figural buratto hand towel. This piece shows excellent workmanship and is very collectible. It is not easy to find pieces like this; however, when you do they are very affordable. Interesting towels like this one are always in demand and prices continue to rise.
Measurements: Overall dimensions: 23"L x 14.5"W
Height of each figure: 5.25"
Collection of: Peggy Zalamea

Chapter 13
Tatting

Tatting evolved from embroidery and is a form of knotted lace consisting of stitches and picots. It is made with cotton or linen thread with a shuttle. In its early evolution, it was used exclusively to decorate other fabrics. However, by the mid-19th century, it became a way of making fabric as well.

Tatting has experienced brief periods of great popularity in Europe and America. The first such period occurred in Europe in the second half of the 18th century. It remained popular until the end of the 18th century, fell into disfavor in the early 19th century before being revived in the mid-19th century when tatting was often used for insertions in cushions and table linen. This revival lasted about twenty years, and tatting did not regain popularity in Europe until the 1920s. The late 1960s saw another brief resurgence in Europe. In the 20th century, Kathleen Warnick and Shirley Nilsson state in their book *Legacy of Lace* that American tatting faded in the 1930s, revived in the 1940s, and disappeared again in the 1960s before reappearing in the 1970s.

Tatting is typically used for edging and insertion purposes as well as in making whole doilies. A wonderful example of a tatted doily is shown in photograph 13.2. Large pieces such as tablecloths and bed covers are almost impossible to find. To date, we have seen only one tatted bed cover.

To the best of our knowledge, tatting is not currently being produced in China. Tatting is currently less expensive than all the needle laces as well as some of the bobbin laces discussed in this book. Good examples are still easy to find. We have not seen any substantial increases in the price of tatting over the last five years and based on current supply and demand, do not anticipate any large appreciation in value any time soon.

13.1 *Origin: U.S.A.*
Date Made: First quarter of the 20th century
Description: A cotton bed sheet with a tatted insertion and border.
Measurements: Overall dimensions: 98"L x 74"W
Collection of: Peggy Zalamea

13.2 Date Made: *Turn of the century*
Description: *A tatted doily, a damask hand towel with tatted ends, and a pair of pillowcases with a tatted border. The damask hand towel has one wide and one narrow band of tatted lace at either end, and two lines of drawnwork at the edge of the hem. The round doily is very fine tatted lace. It is very difficult to find work of this quality.*
Measurements: *Overall dimensions of pillowcase: 31.5"L x 21"W*
Overall dimensions of band towel: 22.5"L x 13.75"W
Diameter of doily: *5"*
Towel and doily, collection of: *Paley Design Center, Philadelphia College of Textiles and Science,*
Gift of: *Miss Frances Peters*
Pillowcases, collection of: *Kay Mertens*

13.3 Origin: *U.S.A.*
Date Made: *First half of the 20th century*
Description: *Four tatted doilies, a linen damask hand towel with a tatted border, a linen runner with a tatted border, a rectangular linen placemat with tatted inserts and border and a square linen mat with a tatted border. All these pieces are easy to find at affordable prices. The most unusual piece in this group is the star-shaped tatted doily with a series of circles in the middle which make it look like a spider's web.*
Measurements: *Overall dimensions of beige doily: 8.5"L x 7.5"W*
Diameter of round white doily: *12.5"*
Diameter of star shaped doily: *8.75"*
Diameter of pink and white doily: *7"*
Overall dimensions of band towel: *24.5"L x 15.25"W*
Overall dimensions of placemat: *17.75"L x 12.25"W*
Overall dimensions of runner: *35"L x 17.5"W*
Overall dimensions of square mat: *14" square*
Collection of: *Peggy Zalamea*

Drawnwork

Drawnwork is a type of embroidery which had its origin in Egypt well before the birth of Christ. For purposes of this book, we will use the term drawnwork to represent both drawn threadwork and pulled threadwork. Drawn threadwork is made by removing selected warp or weft threads from woven fabric, then stitching over the remaining threads with buttonhole or other stitches. Pulled threadwork is made when the threads are not removed but rather when groups of threads are bound together by an overcast stitch, thereby leaving open spaces.

Like cutwork, drawnwork has been used to make all types of household linen. The bulk of modern production is done in China on cotton fabric. Good quality 20th century drawnwork is still well priced. However, early 20th century items are less common than cutwork of the same period. This is partly because drawnwork is often not only more fragile than cutwork but also harder to repair. Large drawnwork pieces such as bed covers and tablecloths in excellent condition are becoming difficult to find. Drawnwork is more popular than cutwork and, as a result, tends to be more expensive than comparable quality cutwork pieces.

Punchwork/Mosaic

Mosaic is a form of drawnwork wherein drawnwork is used to form a series of small, uniformly-sized, open spaces resembling a filet lace net background. The design is formed by the remaining fabric instead of the open spaces. As discussed earlier, the open spaces are what create the pattern in regular drawnwork and cutwork. The open spaces can also be created by using a sharp instrument such as a stiletto to punch small holes in the fabric. The edges of these holes are then covered with an overcast stitch. This type of work is called punchwork. It is often very difficult to tell the difference between drawnwork and punchwork mosaic. Since many people consider all mosaic to be a form of cutwork, it is less popular than other types of drawnwork and commands prices similar to cutwork. Figural punchwork mosaic pieces are not easy to find.

Drawnwork continues to be made today in Europe, North America and China. However, most new pieces do not have the quality or the intricacy of design of the early 20th century pieces. Modern Western pieces tend to be of better quality than those made in China.

14.1 *Origin: Italy*
Date Made: First quarter of the 20th century
Description: A linen figural drawnwork tablecloth with a matching napkin which is one of a set of seven. Each corner of the cloth has a large medallion with six smaller medallions along the sides. A couple of brides have been replaced in one of the medallions. This is an unusual example of drawnwork.
Measurements: Overall dimensions: 120"L x 72"W
Dimensions of large medallions: 18"L x 10.5"W
Dimensions of small medallions: 14.5"L x 8.5"W
Dimensions of napkins: 20" square
Collection of: Peggy Zalamea

14.2 *Date Made: First quarter of the 20th century*
Description: A linen drawnwork bed cover with Tenerife lace
inserts. Drawnwork pieces typically have the drawnwork interspersed
with untouched portions of fabric. This piece is highly unusual because
it is completely made of drawnwork. Linen fabric is the most commonly
used material for this type of drawnwork. Cotton is less common and
silk is very rare.
Measurements: Overall dimensions: 90"L x 74"W
Collection of: Peggy Zalamea

14.3 *Origin: Italy*
Date Made: First half of the 20th century
Description: A figural punchwork mosaic bed sheet and sham with
machine embroidery made of cotton. The workmanship is average
however the subject matter (cherubs) and the size of the sheet make it
collectible. The fact that it is a set also adds to the value.
Measurements: Overall dimensions of sheet: 101"L x 94"W
Overall dimensions of sham: 27.5"L x 90"W
Average size of cherubs: 5"H x 3.5"W
Collection of: Peggy Zalamea

14.4 *Origin: Italy*
Date Made: First half of the 20th century
Description: A linen punchwork mosaic bed sheet and a pair of
similar pillowcases each made of linen. The workmanship on both
pieces is very fine. In many newer pieces, too little thread is used so the
raw edges of the punched out holes can still be seen. In both these pieces,
the thread is densely packed and the stitching is very even.
Measurements: Overall dimensions of sheet: 93"L x 68"W
Overall dimensions of pillowcase: 33"L x 20"W
Collection of: Peggy Zalamea

14.5 Origin: Italy

Date Made: First quarter of the 20th century

Description: A linen punchwork mosaic and buratto oval tablecloth.
Large oval tablecloths are hard to find. In addition, the workmanship
and the quality in this cloth are wonderful. The punchwork holes vary
in size to add even more interest to the overall design. A more typical
punchwork cloth would have holes of uniform size throughout the
design. Even the two monograms have been made with punchwork.
Monograms are more typically embroidered after the piece has been
made. The monograms on this cloth were obviously made at the same
time as the cloth, which means that it was custom made.

Measurements: Overall dimensions of sheet: 68"L x 132"W

Overall dimensions of monogram medallion: 8"L x 6.50"W

Collection of: Peggy Zalamea

14.6 *Date Made: First half of the 20th century*
Description: Two linen punchwork placemats, two linen
punchwork napkins and a figural linen punchwork runner. Both
napkins are part of sets of six. The set with butterflies is less common
than the set with a floral theme. All five pieces are very good quality and
are good examples of punchwork. The most collectible piece is the
runner which has six animals in its design. None of these pieces except
for the runner are expensive, and all these pieces are easy to find.

Measurements: Overall dimensions of oval placemat: 14"L x 10"W
Overall dimensions of rectangular placemat: 16.5"L x 11"W
Overall dimensions of napkin with butterfly: 12" square
Overall dimensions of other napkin: 13.5" x 13"
Overall dimensions of runner: 24.5"L x 14.5"W
Dimensions of figural squares in runner: 2.25" square
Two placemats and one napkin, collection of: Elizabeth Scofield
Runner and figural napkin, collection of: Peggy Zalamea

14.7 Date Made: *First half of the 20th century*
Description: A linen punchwork runner and napkins. The runner is
very good quality with fine embroidery to enhance the punchwork
design. The napkins are from a set of eight. Each has a punchwork
design in one of the four corners. Both the runner and the set of napkins
are easy to find and very affordable.
Measurements: Overall dimensions of runner: 46"L x 16.5"W
Overall dimensions of napkins: 16.5" square
Collection of: Elizabeth Scofield

14.8 *Date Made: First half of the 20th century*
Description: A linen napkin with a drawnwork design in one corner.
This napkin is one from a set of eight. This type of napkin is difficult to
find in sets of eight or more.
Measurements: Overall dimensions: 24" square
Collection of: Elizabeth Scofield

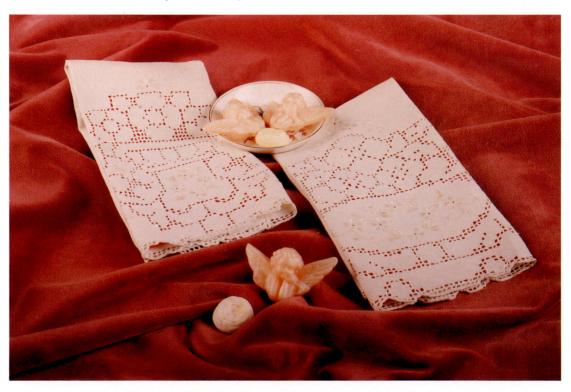

14.9 *Date Made: Second half of the 20th century*
Description: A pair of cotton punchwork hand towels with embroidery.
These towels are easy to locate and will make a lovely addition to your
powder room.
Measurements: Overall Dimensions: 20.5"L x 14"W
Collection of: Elizabeth Scofield

14.10 Origin: *China*
Date Made: *First half of the 20th century*
Descriptions: *A drawnwork linen tea cloth with an embroidered dragon
in the center. This linen is loosely woven and very brittle. Many of the
household linens made with this fabric that we have seen have tears
along the fold lines. Pieces like this are not easy to find in good
condition. The workmanship is good. Large pieces with this dragon
motif are popular and command relatively high prices.*
Measurements: *Overall dimensions: 46"L x 44"W*
Dimensions of dragon: *18"L x 17"W*
Collection of: *Roger Crockett*

Market Conditions

Economic Factors

As with all other antiques and collectibles, vintage linens and lace prices are affected by the state of local and world economies. Although the long term trend for vintage linens and lace prices is up, there are short term downturns in prices that usually coincide with economic recessions. Antiques and collectibles are a luxury fewer people can afford in a recession when disposable incomes are shrinking.

Most of the 1980s saw tremendous increases in disposable incomes as well as record prices in many areas of collecting. However, the late 1980s and early 1990s saw weak economies in many parts of the world with a record number of bankruptcies and high unemployment in the United States and correspondingly sharp declines in the prices of many antiques and collectibles. It should be noted that the hardest hit were items of mediocre or low quality. Anything that was rare and/or of excellent quality continued to sell well and, in some cases, at record prices even during the depths of the recession. With an economic recovery underway, prices should start to rebound in even the hardest hit segments of the antiques and collectibles markets.

A Prime Time To Buy

Even after taking into account price declines during the recent recession, many 20th century collectibles are worth considerably more today than they were ten years ago. Costume jewelry is a prime example. Women who refused to wear costume jewelry ten years ago now boast of their collections of Miriam Haskell, Hobe, and Eisenberg costume jewelry.

Although prices for vintage linens and lace have experienced sizeable increases during the same period, they do not begin to compare with the price increases in the costume jewelry market. One major reason for this is that fashion can dramatically affect prices even in an economic downturn. Women tend to buy more jewelry and less clothing in a recession. This was true in the Great Depression, as evidenced by the large quantities of 1930s jewelry available today. Household linens, however, are viewed as an expense that can be deferred. As a result, 20th century linens and lace are still undiscovered and underpriced! Prices for some of the rarer pieces have started to climb into eyebrow-raising territory, but there is a great deal of room for further appreciation even at the top end of the market. The vast majority of 20th century linens and lace are readily available at very affordable prices. Great bargains are still available to collectors who are willing to spend the time searching for them.

Recently, Liz visited one of the best known flea markets in the United States where she purchased a beautiful crocheted bed cover in perfect condition for $50.00 late in the day. On the day she purchased it, the bed cover probably could have been sold for up to $225.00 at another venue. The fact that she was able to do this so late in the day illustrates our point. It is unlikely that a great piece of costume jewelry, a collectible toy, or a wonderful German doll, priced at a fraction of its value, would still have been available an hour after the market opened because there are a tremendous number of knowledgeable collectors for these items.

We both continue to find similar bargains on a regular basis. However, these market conditions are not likely to last forever. For a variety of reasons discussed below, we feel that the 20th century linens and lace market is poised for a boom.

Demand is on the Rise

There are a relatively small number of dealers who sell antique and vintage linens and lace exclusively, with a correspondingly small pool of serious collectors. However, both of these groups are growing. There is a growing awareness and appreciation of old textiles in general and linens and lace in particular. This has been fueled by museum exhibitions, a plethora of new books, magazines, and other reading material on the subject. Another factor affecting demand is that more and more people are realizing that early 20th century linens and lace are a good value. They sell at a discount compared to new items. For instance, wonderful Italian embroidered linen bed sheets made in the 1920s currently sell for under $100.00. On a recent trip to Venice, Peggy saw new plain linen bed sheets with very simple drawnwork borders priced at over $500.00!

The Supply Continues to Decrease

The available pool of very fine examples of early 20th century pieces was never very large. A few years ago, Liz was fortunate enough to purchase a rectangular linen tablecloth with filet and needle lace inserts made in Italy in the 1920s from a lady who still had the original receipt. The cloth had been purchased from John Wanamaker in Philadelphia for $100.00. Since there were very few people who could afford to spend this much money on one tablecloth at that time, it is logical to assume that very few of these tablecloths were made and sold then.

At the same time, the available pool of collectible linens and lace continues to shrink for a number of reasons:

1) Although there are exceptions, textiles are more easily damaged than most other collectibles. The vast majority of household linens were meant for everyday use resulting in extensive wear and tear. For instance, curtains hung on exterior windows were constantly exposed to sunlight, which causes fading and disintegration of fibers. Bed and table linen require frequent washing. Modern washing techniques can be very stressful -detergents, bleaches, and washing machines are all very harsh on old textiles.

2) Many textiles are also damaged by improper storage. This topic will be covered extensively in the care and maintenance section of this book.

3) Once a piece has been damaged, finding people capable of repairing it is very difficult.

4) The remaining stock of old linens and lace is being further reduced by people adapting old pieces to fit their current lifestyles. For instance, many old banquet-size linen damask tablecloths, for place settings of twelve or more, have been cut up to fit tables seating six or less, which are more common in these days of apartment living and smaller families. Partly as a result of this practice, banquet tablecloths have become quite scarce.

5) Some wonderful lace is still being made in Europe today but certainly not in enough quantity to replace the older pieces that are being damaged or destroyed every day. It is simply not economically feasible to make large quantities of high quality lace today. It takes too long to make. Ernst Erik Pfannschmidt writes on page 9 in his book *20th Century Lace* that "In 1942, a triangular [lace] mantilla was made for the Milan Tiennale. It was worked in black silk and measured 1.20 metres by 2.60 metres (47 1/2 by 102 1/2 in.). It took three women one year and six months. The mantilla was worked in three parts which were subsequently joined with invisible lace stitches. It weighed 100 grammes (little more than 3 oz.). It was designed by Professor Franco Bossi, who designed for the bobbin lace school of Cantu." If this same piece were made today in the United States by three women paid at the minimum wage rate of $ 4.25/hour, working eight hours a day, five days a week for one year and six months (seventy-eight weeks), the total cost of labor alone would be $39,780.00. How many could afford this piece today? For this reason, many larger items, such as handmade needle lace tablecloths seating at least twelve people, are not readily available today and can only be custom ordered at prohibitive cost.

The Chinese continue to produce large quantities of handmade copies of some types of European linens and lace. While many of these pieces are of good quality, they typically do not begin to rival the older as well as more current European pieces in terms of quality, intricacy and complexity of design. A coarser thread is typically used to produce relatively simple designs. In our opinion, these pieces are not collectible and will not affect the market for collectible 20th century household linens and lace by increasing the supply.

The prices of new Italian *point de venise* versus new Chinese *point de venise* certainly reflect this difference in quality. The former can run into the thousands of dollars whereas the latter can be obtained for several hundred dollars or less. Early 20th century Chinese copies of European figural lace are becoming collectible but are still a fraction of the cost of Western European lace.

We recently found some linen cocktail napkins with very simple drawnwork bearing the original paper labels "Made in Occupied Japan". In addition, some machine-made copies of European lace have been produced in Japan. The Japanese copies are not as good as the Chinese ones and are not collectible at this time. Currently, the bulk of production in Asia comes from The People's Republic of China, Hong Kong, and the Philippines.

Rising demand, coupled with shrinking supply, should lead to increasing upward pressure on prices; hence, our conclusion that this is a prime time to buy for the beginning as well as the experienced collector.

The Art of Collecting

It is always fun to ask dealers and collectors how they acquired their interest. In Liz's case it began with her grandmother. When Liz was a child her grandmother, who was a master of crochet and embroidery, created beautiful linens for their home. The curtains in the house were lace and most of the household linens were adorned with embroidery and crochet. Although Liz envied her grandmother's talent, she never acquired her skills. Most of Liz's efforts at embroidery were hidden in the linen closet while her efforts at crochet never even made it that far. As is the case with many families, none of her grandmother's linens were passed on to other family members, so they are now just memories. Liz was about thirty before she decided to acquire the kind of linens that figured prominently in her childhood memories, and she has been collecting ever since.

Peggy, on the other hand, fell into textile collecting by accident. She was in the process of renovating and furnishing a late 19th century house. While at a major New York antique show, looking for antique silver and china for her dining room, she saw a beautiful lace tablecloth draped at the rear of Liz's booth. She fell in love with it and bought it without knowing anything about lace. In the process of finding out more about this tablecloth (photograph 11.13), she became interested in antique and collectible linens and lace and has been actively collecting ever since. This tablecloth was part of Liz's collection, and she likes to check on it occasionally to make sure Peggy is taking care of it.

There are a few general guidelines that the beginning collector should follow:

Education: Preparation for the Search

It is important to study linens and lace before beginning a collection. This is especially true if you hope to acquire a collection which will appreciate in value over the years.

Begin to educate yourself in the area(s) of your interest by reading, visiting museums, talking to knowledgeable people in the field, and seeing and handling as many items as possible to teach yourself the difference between good, bad, and merely mediocre examples of antique and collectible linens and lace. This research phase should cover not only teaching yourself to identify different types of linens and lace, particularly the difference between machine-made and handmade, but it should also encourage the development of a good sense of what the market prices are for things that are easy to find versus things that are rare.

Read Books

The following are some good reference books on linens and lace:

Legacy of Lace by Kathleen Warnick and Shirley Nilsson
The Identification of Lace by Pat Earnshaw
Lace, A Guide to Identification of Old Lace Types and Techniques by Heather Toomer

During the course of your research, you may find that some of the reference books you read sometimes contradict each other. Don't be discouraged. Books, and indeed any other reference materials, are most effective when used together with the other sources of information mentioned in this chapter.

Visit Museums

There are many museums in the United States and Canada that have prestigious linens and lace collections. We have listed a few of them below. When planning a visit to any museum be sure to call ahead regarding the days and hours the linens and lace exhibits are open. In many cases the textile collections in museums are open to the public by appointment only.

If you are interested in using the research facilities of a museum, we advise you to write to the museum to make an appointment. Please be as specific as possible when making a request to view items that are not on exhibit. Linda Cheetham has written a booklet entitled *The Innocent Researcher and the Museum*, which is a useful guide to the do's and don'ts when using museum research facilities.

The Art Institute of Chicago
Michigan Avenue at Adams Street
Chicago, Illinois 60603
(312) 443-3696

Brooklyn Museum
Eastern Parkway and Washington Street
Brooklyn, NY 11238
(718) 638-5000

Cooper-Hewitt Museum
The Smithsonian Institution's National Museum of
    Design

2 East 91st Street
New York, NY 10028
(212) 860-6868

The Metropolitan Museum of Art
Fifth Avenue (at 82nd Street)
New York, NY 10028
(212) 570-3711
(The Metropolitan Museum of Art has one of the largest and most important collections of lace in the world. As of the writing of this book, its lace collection numbered over 5,000 pieces.)

Hillwood Museum
4155 Linnear Ave. N.W.
Washington, DC 20008
(202) 686-5807

Rhode Island School of Design
224 Benefit Street
Providence, RI 02903
(401) 454-6514

The Lace Museum
552 South Murphy
Sunnyvale, CA 94086
(408) 730-4695

The Museum for Textiles
55 Centre Avenue
Toronto, ONT M5G 2H5
(416) 599-5515

The Royal Ontario Museum
100 Queen's Park
Toronto, ONT
(416) 586-5551

Consult Dealers

Reputable dealers can also be very good sources of information. There are several reasons for this. Many dealers, including the authors, started off as collectors before becoming dealers. Rarely will you meet a collector who doesn't enjoy talking about his or her collection or field of interest and a collector/dealer is no different. At the same time, it is in the dealer's best interest to have an educated customer. Reputable dealers are not interested in cheating customers to make a quick profit. They are interested in developing long-term relationships with clients and one of the best ways to do this is by ensuring that their clients can recognize excellent or good quality items when they see them and understand why things are priced the way they are. Twentieth century household linen can be purchased in today's market for a few dollars or a few thousand dollars; and if you can't tell the difference between a $10.00 piece versus a $1,000.00 piece, you will be a very difficult customer.

Having said all these wonderful things about the good dealers, we do not want you to assume that all dealers are experts on all aspects of linens and lace. For instance, we have met dealers who specialize in plain bed linen and have absolutely no interest or expertise in lace. It is important for you to talk to several dealers and judge for yourself which ones are knowledgeable and honest. We should also point out that even the best dealers do make mistakes. It is your judgment that counts in the final analysis, and this is why educating yourself is so important.

Incidentally, your quest for knowledge should never really end. We do not profess to know everything there is to know about linens and lace and are constantly discovering new things. In addition, even though over time we have developed sources that we go to regularly, we find that it is still a good idea to visit other sources from time to time to gain a better perspective on the market as a whole. For example, it would be best to periodically recheck the offerings among the respective dealers in your area to determine shifts in price and selection.

Tools of the Trade

In order for your own search for linens and lace to be productive and fun, you must be prepared with the proper tools. We always carry a jeweler's loupe or magnifying glass, a tape measure at least fifteen feet long, a flashlight, and paper and pen. The magnifying glass is of great help when you are trying to decide whether a piece is handmade or machine-made and when you are trying to determine the quality of the piece. Many dealers and auction houses do not list the measurements of pieces they are selling. Therefore, if you are looking for a specific size to fit your bed, dining table or window, you should have a tape measure handy. Your search will often take you to places that are not very well lit; hence, the need for a flashlight. And finally, unless you have an excellent memory, you will need a pad and pen to take notes on the things in which you have an interest. This is of particular importance when inspecting items at auction, as you will see later in this chapter.

Where to Buy - Sources

It is difficult to predict where collectors might find excellent examples of antique and collectible household linen. Our collections were acquired from antique shops, antique shows, antique textile shops, auctions, estates, flea markets, friends' linen closets, house sales and thrift shops. We both love to shop, so very few sources have escaped our joint efforts.

All collectors have stories to tell about items found in totally unexpected places, items that turn out to be worth significantly more than they paid for them, or items that they bought that they thought were one thing but turned out to be something completely different. For instance, a few years ago, Liz found a very nice large, handmade army/navy tablecloth at a flea market that was being used by an antique dealer to cover the top of her display table. The dealer, who was a jewelry dealer and not a linen dealer, thought the tablecloth was a cheap machine-made piece and was very surprised when Liz offered to buy it. Liz paid $85.00 for the cloth, which may have sold for as much as $450.00 at another place.

Sources: Flea Markets and Antique Shows

Flea markets usually offer a mix of things old and new. They are a prime source for buying undervalued items. Antique shows, on the other hand, are geared to offering the best items dealers have, and the prices are usually close to current market value. Antique shows are more likely to cover a specific period and/or type of merchandise. There are shows devoted to antique textiles and clothing, vintage textiles and clothing, stamps and coins, or Victoriana, just to name a few examples.

The concept of "vetting" an antique show is quite common in Europe and is starting to catch on in the United States. "Vetting" refers to the practice of show organizers bringing in a team of experts to check items for sale in the show to ensure that the sellers are correctly describing their merchandise in terms of details such as date made, place of origin, and degree of restoration. A "vetted" show will be advertised as such. "Vetting" is not done at flea markets. Please note that many items sold at flea markets are sold "as is" on a cash basis. This is one more reason why prices at flea markets are often cheaper than those at antique shows.

When shopping at flea markets or antique shows, it is important to get there early. In the antique world, the "early bird" almost always gets the bargains and the rare items.

It is generally a good idea to ask dealers at flea markets and antique shows if they have other items not yet on display. If you are looking for something specific, such as bed sheets, you can save some time by asking the dealer if he or she has any. Many dealers keep their best pieces hidden because they don't want to risk having them damaged. They only bring them out if they think a customer is a serious buyer and/or the type who would appreciate the beauty of the piece. Other dealers simply don't have the space to display everything and end up leaving quite a bit of stock in boxes which they will allow you to look through. Still others keep things for special customers. If the latter is the case, you may be lucky and convince the dealer to sell to you instead. For instance, Peggy was at a flea market in London, England, talking to a dealer who had a wonderful assortment of linen. This dealer saw that Peggy really was interested in beautiful linen and started taking out even more spectacular things from a small cupboard. After buying a few pieces, Peggy mentioned that she was looking for old pillowcases and sheets. The dealer happened to have a stash of pillowcases that she was holding for a client. Apparently, the client was in the habit of stopping by every few weeks to look through the pillowcases and pay for the ones she wanted. She almost always bought the dealer's entire pillowcase inventory and was clearly a very good customer. Nevertheless, the dealer let Peggy look through this stash, and she ended up with a very nice pair of Victorian drawnwork linen shams in mint condition.

Sources: Antique Shops

Most antique shops carry a wide range of merchandise from the very expensive to the highly affordable. However, merchandise found in shops tends to be more expensive than that found in flea markets. Prices are more comparable to those in antique shows. Bargains can still be found but you are more likely to pay market prices.

Reputable antique shops give guarantees on all merchandise sold. Some shop owners may also let you take things "on approval" for a short period of time. This means if you're not sure if a piece will fit or whether the color will match, you can take it home on a trial basis. Most dealers will give you one or two days before you either have to return the piece or buy it.

Sources: Buying at Auction

When buying at auction, you should keep several things in mind. Trustees often consign whole estates to auction houses to sell. The best of the items from these estates are sold individually. The odds and ends that are deemed to be of little value are assigned by type to boxes to make them easier and more economical to sell. Just think how awful it would be to watch someone auctioning off hundreds of items for a dollar each!

Most auction houses still don't pay much attention to the linens and lace. They usually don't have an in-house expert, they don't advertise them, and they don't display them. Therefore, examine the boxes carefully and don't be embarrassed to bring out your flashlight if the boxes are located in a very dark corner of the auction house.

A few years ago, Peggy saw a wonderful box of linen, which had a very low estimate, go for a then unheard of price of well over $1,000.00. Two furniture dealers sitting behind her were clearly perplexed at all the interest. One of them asked his companion, "What's in the box — gold?" Peggy was amused to note that soon after that auction that particular auction house started selling large linen and lace pieces individually with much higher estimates. Their estimates had been $10.00 to $50.00 per box. Their new estimates were typically $100.00 to $300.00 per piece! Unfortunately, they obviously thought that size was the determining factor in setting the estimates because they used the same estimate for a large crocheted tablecloth and a linen cutwork tablecloth. After you have read the price section of this book, you will see that there is a big difference in price between these two types of items.

Auction house catalogues do not list the contents of boxes of linens and lace, so it is your responsibility to remember what is in a box if you intend to bid on it. There are usually several boxes in any given auction, and various pieces have a mysterious way of migrating from box to box during the exhibition period. Some people inspecting the contents may unintentionally, if the boxes are side by side, return the items to the wrong box. Others engage in the dishonest and obnoxious practice of "salting" boxes. This means that they move the items they are interested in to another box that contains items of considerably less value. They then bid on the latter, hoping that no one has noticed the switch so that they can acquire the valuable items at a very low price. Other unsuspecting people pay higher prices for the boxes that originally contained the valuable pieces only to find, when they pick up their boxes after the auction, that they have paid a sizeable amount of money for a box that contains only junk. We have both bought boxes which turned out to be missing some or even all the pieces we were interested in purchasing.

There is nothing you can do to eliminate "migration". However, you can minimize the problem by doing two things. You should (a) inspect the box(es) you intend to bid on just prior to the auction and bid on the box that contains the items you are interested in and (b) pick up your box(es) as soon as possible. Many auction houses state quite clearly that responsibility for the item transfers to the buyer when the auctioneer bangs his gavel down and says "sold". This is not a problem in auction houses where all items that are sold are kept in a secure area until the buyers can pick them up. However, other auction houses leave things lying around the room where the auction is conducted, which means items you have bought are accessible to everyone. We both know of instances where unscrupulous people have walked off with other people's purchases. If you find yourself in a situation where you are either missing pieces out of your box(es) or unable to locate your box(es) at all, your best bet is to talk to the auctioneer and hope that he will refund your money. An auctioneer refunded Peggy's money on one occasion when she was unable to recover some items. However, it was through sheer luck because the catalogue description listed three tablecloths when the box clearly contained only two. Please keep in mind that auctioneers can't possibly remember the exact contents of every boxed lot; so, without a precise description in the catalogue, it is almost impossible for you to prove that you are missing things from your box. If the auctioneer has never seen you before, he has no way of judging whether or not you are telling the truth. After all, it is not unheard of for people to get carried away during the bidding and then try to get out of paying when their euphoria has worn off. We have heard many stories from others who have not been so lucky and have not been able to get either the items back or their money refunded.

When inspecting items, particularly at auction, pay close attention to the condition of the pieces. Reputable dealers will usually point out stains, holes, tears, and restoration. They may also be able to give you an estimate on the cost of any repairs you may wish to have done. However, auction houses, which work on much thinner spreads and much higher volume, simply do not have the manpower to be as meticulous on every single lot they sell. Consequently, when dealing with boxed lots, many auction houses will tell you that they are selling the items "as is". One other thing to remember when buying at auction is that many people will handle the linens during the viewing period. Linens and lace are quite fragile and should be handled with care. Unfortunately, not everyone will handle them properly. For this reason, it is a good idea to inspect the pieces you wish to bid on just before the auction starts so that you will be able to see if any damage was done to the pieces during the viewing.

All of the above may have led you to conclude that buying from auction houses can be a risky proposition, and you may be wondering why anyone would buy from an auction house instead of from a reputable dealer. The main reason is price. Although the lines have blurred considerably over the past few years, you should still, theoretically, be paying wholesale prices at auction and retail prices to dealers. Please note that we said theoretically; you should not automatically assume that auction prices will always be cheaper. You should be aware of what average retail prices and average auction prices are for the items you are interested in so that you don't end up paying more at auction than you would have if you bought directly from a dealer. Some auction houses put estimates in their catalogues to assist potential buyers. We caution you against placing much faith in these estimates. As mentioned earlier, most auction houses don't know much about linen, and we have rarely found their estimates to be very accurate.

Sources: Thrift Shops

It is a good idea to shop at thrift shops on a regular basis. Families often donate household linen to them when a family member dies or when the family is moving and is in the process of cleaning out the attic and basement. They are also a prime source for consignment merchandise. In general, prices are below full retail but well above those found at flea markets.

Sources: House Sales/Tag Sales

House sales, which are also known as tag sales, are usually advertised in local newspapers. They often include linens and lace at quite reasonable prices. Many of the people who run house and tag sales are unfamiliar with the market for collectible linens and lace.

Condition

Linens and lace should be carefully examined before they are purchased. Small flaws can have a considerable effect on the price of 20th century items. Breaks in the brides, pin holes, rips and stains all affect the value of an item. This is particularly important if you are interested in the investment potential of a piece. It should be noted that minor flaws are less of a factor when dealing with rare pieces. Stains and other minor flaws are a fact of life when dealing with older textiles. They are a part of the textiles' social history. You will severely limit your collection if you wish to buy only older pieces that look like new. However, condition should play a greater role in your decision making when you are considering a piece which is easy to find in excellent condition. Although there are exceptions, items that have been reduced in size or changed in some way are also less valuable than items that are all original. It is interesting to note that in Europe, where there is a long history of antique textile collecting, stains are less of a factor than they are in North America. Some stains, however, are hard to spot in artificial light. It is much easier to spot stains in sunlight. It is also easier to spot small holes in woven fabric by holding the piece up with strong light behind it. The light will shine through any holes.

The following is a guide we use to classify pieces according to their condition:

Excellent - Minimal or no damage. Minimal is defined as minor stains or detached brides which are easy to reattach. The latter is a common condition in larger lace pieces because the weight of the thread often causes the brides to detach when the piece is being handled. As long as the brides are not completely missing in a large piece of lace, they should not be a factor in your decision. The only exception to this is chemical lace where brides are very difficult to reattach. Detached brides in chemical lace would lower the valuation of the piece. Minor stains are defined as stains so faint as to be impossible to see except in strong sunlight.

Good - One or two pinholes in the fabric, minor stains, brides detached, a few brides missing. The piece is considered good even if more than one of these problems exists in the same piece.

Fair - More than two pinholes in the fabric, some missing pieces of lace, repaired portions of lace and/or fabric, very noticeable stains, some fraying of edges of woven fabric.

Poor - Damaged beyond salvaging. Useful only for cutting up and incorporating into something else.

Monograms

You should also take into consideration whether or not you can live with someone else's monogrammed initials. Many beautiful pieces, particularly bed and table linens, have monograms on them. If you don't care if there is a monogram, you will have a much wider selection to choose from than someone who cares about the monogram. It's not a big problem for people with common initials who will only buy a monogrammed piece if it matches their initials. However, if you have a last name beginning with Z as Peggy does, monograms become a big problem. Many collectors don't mind monograms. They believe people may assume that a monogrammed piece that doesn't match their initials was simply inherited from a relative. In addition, monograms can be works of art in their own right that contribute to rather than detract from the beauty of a piece. However, if you are at all worried about investment or resale value, we should point out that dealers usually have an easier time selling pieces without monograms. As in the case of condition, monograms on a rare piece have less of an impact on price.

Negotiating Prices

The rule of thumb is to negotiate more aggressively on routine pieces as opposed to scarce items. Always be sensible and honorable when negotiating prices. Whenever possible, bargain privately and not within hearing distance of other buyers. A discount of ten to fifteen percent on a scarce item is fair as long as the item isn't severely overpriced. Some of the scarce items in today's market are:

- large round linen and/or lace tablecloths seating at least six people
- large figural filet lace items
- linen bed sheets with embroidery, embroidered cutwork, or lace insertions with matching pillowcases (especially queen and king size)
- sets of twelve or more old cutwork linen dinner napkins with filet lace or needle lace inserts, (new napkins are being made in China but are smaller, of lesser quality and usually in cotton)
- Western European needle lace tablecloths of all sizes
- sets of eight or more lace placemats (especially figural) with or without matching dinner napkins and/or runners
- most Appenzell and Appenzell-type pieces (especially large figural tablecloths with or without matching napkins)

You should also be aware that pairs of certain types of items sell for more when sold as a pair instead of separately. Pairs of pillowcases are a classic example. If the pair of cases sold for $ 65.00, the same pillowcases when sold separately would only be worth $ 10.00 to $15.00 each. In addition, a set of napkins is worth less if each napkin is sold individually. Interestingly enough, with the exception of rare types of lace or embroidery, matching sets consisting of a runner, a set of placemats and a set of napkins are often worth more if the three major components are sold separately. Dealers break up the sets to make them more affordable. This is one of the reasons why matching sets are becoming quite scarce. Many dealers will actually give you a discount if you are willing to buy all three major components at the same time. Tablecloths with matching sets of napkins made of the types of lace or embroidery that are easy to find are also worth more if the tablecloth is sold separately from the napkins.

Seller's Return Policy

Regardless of where you buy, you should always check on the seller's policy on returns. As discussed earlier, some sell items "as is" with absolutely no guarantees regarding when or where the piece was made, what type of lace it is, or condition. Others allow you to return things within a certain

period of time. Others give full guarantees with no expiration, provided you return the piece in the same condition as when you purchased it.

Many dealers at flea markets do not have shops, so trying to get in touch with them to return defective merchandise can be difficult. Dealers at antique shows that do not have shops should still be willing to guarantee their merchandise. Make sure you get a detailed receipt and the dealer's business card so you have some way to get in touch with him if there is a problem.

Upgrading Your Collection

As discussed earlier, the best examples of any type of antique or collectible hold their value better in a recession and usually appreciate more rapidly when prices in general are on an upswing. Therefore, it is a good practice to buy the best you can afford. It is better to spend $100.00 on one good piece than $100.00 on ten damaged or mediocre pieces. In addition, it is advisable to sell items from your collection when better examples become available. For instance, let's assume you have a *point de venise* placemat in your collection. Two years after you purchased it, you find a set of figural *point de venise* placemats that you can afford. A set is more valuable than a single placemat if the quality of the workmanship is comparable. In addition, a figural placemat is more desirable than a placemat with a more common floral theme. After you have purchased the set, we recommend that you sell the single placemat, thereby freeing up additional funds to buy something else for your collection.

Useful Measurements to Know

When shopping for household linens, there are some useful measurements to keep in mind.

If you don't have precise measurements for your dining table and are trying to figure out how long a tablecloth you need, you can do a rough calculation by allowing two feet per place setting plus a twelve to fifteen inch overhang on each end. In the early part of this century, some books recommended an eight to twelve inch overhang for a luncheon cloth as opposed to twelve to fifteen inches for a dinner cloth. Luncheon napkins are thirteen to eighteen inches square while dinner napkins should be twenty-two to twenty-eight inches square.

If you don't have precise measurements for your windows, it helps to keep in mind that if you want the curtains to drop to the floor, standard windows in 20th century houses require curtains that are at least eighty-four inches long.

Pricing

There are very few sources on pricing antique and collectible household linens. Even the most widely read antique review books do not include extensive coverage of linen and lace prices. Hopefully, this book will help establish a benchmark for pricing and make it easier for more people to take an active interest in collecting these wonderful works of art from our past.

As in all collecting, the relative scarcity of an item greatly influences its price. We began our collections by purchasing the rarest items we could find. We did this because we felt that as linen and lace collecting became more popular, these items would increase in value more rapidly than easier to find items. Our theory has proved true, not just for textile collecting, but for all other areas of collecting as well.

Household linens and lace were made primarily in white or ecru. However, the entire color spectrum has also been used. Does color affect price? The answer is a qualified yes. Color is not a factor in very rare pieces but does play a role in determining prices for most other household linens and lace. Some colors, such as green, have traditionally been less popular. White has consistently been the most popular, with ecru coming in a distant second. If you had two pieces that were identical in every respect except color, assuming one piece was white and the other was not, the white piece would probably sell more quickly and at a higher price. Please note that there are some exceptions. For instance, colored linen damask is currently in greater demand than white linen damask. As discussed elsewhere in this book, fashion affects demand; colors that are popular today may be out of fashion next year. While it is difficult to imagine white ever going out of fashion, changes in fashion could cause minor fluctuations in the prices of colored household linens and lace.

It is important for the reader to note that geographics, median income, and collector preferences which vary from one area to another, all significantly influence price as well. Crocheted items, for instance, appear to command higher prices in the U.S. Midwest. Large sets of linen damask dinner napkins and large lace tablecloths sell best in large urban centers where formal entertaining is common. Colored embroidery on white or colored fabrics sell better at country auctions than at city auctions.

In the United States, the most elaborate and expensive lace pieces are most often sold in the South in cities like Atlanta and on the East Coast in cities like New York, Baltimore, and Washington D.C. In Canada, top prices are paid in Ottawa, Toronto, and Montreal. Ottawa, in its capacity as the capital of Canada, is the center of the country's diplomatic social scene. Formal entertaining is common there which means there is a strong demand for high quality linen.

Although there are exceptions, vintage linens and lace tend to sell at higher prices in the U.S. vis à vis Canada. This is largely a function of the difference in size between the populations of these two countries. The U.S. has a population of approximately two hundred fifty million people, whereas Canada has only twenty-five million people. Consequently, there are many more collectors for all types of antiques and collectibles in the U.S.

Prices are even higher in Western Europe, and many European antique textile dealers come to North America to shop. We have noticed that, on many occasions, a piece that sells in Canada for $10.00 Canadian would sell in the United States for $10.00 U.S. and in England for ten British Pounds. Since the Canadian dollar is lower than the U.S. dollar, which in turn is lower than the British Pound, the piece actually sells for considerably more in England than it does in Canada.

Investment Potential

Most buyers of earlier 20th century household linens and lace are looking for something decorative and/or useful for their homes at an affordable price. Very few think of their pieces as items that could appreciate in value in the future. Peggy recently bought a whole collection of good quality Irish linen damask towels, linen placemats, and other small linen pieces from an elderly lady. The collection had been accumulating in her attic for years. As various relatives died or moved away, unwanted linens somehow ended up in this lady's attic. This woman was astonished that anyone would actually give her money for these unwanted bits and pieces. Unfortunately, this lady is not alone in thinking of 20th century linens and lace as "junk". An old school friend of Peggy's called her recently because he had heard that she was in the antique business. He was interested in acquiring some 18th century English furniture and was flabbergasted to find that Peggy specialized in textiles. He associated linens and lace with garage sales. He, like many others, did not realize how much time and effort goes into making even the most inexpensive of linens, such as a tatted doily that would sell for under $10.00.

When buying a new linen piece, such as a bed sheet, you should be aware that if you tried to sell that piece in the next ten years, you would probably only receive a fraction of what you paid for it. However, earlier 20th century linens and lace stand a much better chance of holding their value. Consequently, while investment potential should not be the primary consideration when collecting 20th century linens and lace, or any other antiques or collectibles, you should, nevertheless, be aware that the potential for appreciation is there. If you are interested in the investment aspect of 20th century household linens and lace, there are four basic rules to follow:

a) Collect rare pieces. As discussed earlier, rare pieces tend to appreciate in value more rapidly than pieces that are readily available. This is true even if the piece is slightly damaged.

b) When possible, collect pieces in excellent condition. As discussed earlier, pieces which are readily available stand a much better chance of appreciating in value if they are in excellent condition. Condition is less important when you are dealing with a rare piece.

c) Never rule out taste when collecting for investment. Try to be on the forefront of changes in consumer taste. Any sudden change in consumer taste can turn the investment potential of an item upside down. For example, if the First Lady decided that only collectible crochet tablecloths were to be used at the White House for state occasions, the crochet tablecloth market would immediately skyrocket.

d) Document provenance. When possible, obtain a history of ownership and other pertinent information when pieces are purchased for your collection.

Peggy's brother-in-law is fond of saying that you're really not getting a good deal if you buy something you don't want or need just because it's cheap. At the same time you shouldn't buy something simply because it's rare. It doesn't matter how many people tell you that something is a fabulous piece that you won't see for another fifty years. The deciding factor should be whether you like it or not. After all, you are the one who will have to live with what you buy. At a major New York antique show a few years ago, Liz felt that the best piece of lace in the show was a rare, figural lace tablecloth dominated by enormous filet lace cherubs. The workmanship was superb and the condition was excellent. The $2,000.00 price tag was rather high but not unreasonable for the piece. Peggy was looking for something like it for her collection but did not buy this piece because she didn't like the way the cherubs looked. She felt that the long, thin cherubs looked as if they were starving and she knew she wouldn't be able to see them every day without feeling sorry for them. Liz couldn't believe it! After all, you don't get too many opportunities to buy something of this quality. However, while the investment aspect is not unimportant, it is secondary to the aesthetic aspect for both of us. For those of you who do care more about the investment side, we would still advise you to buy what you like. You can't be right one hundred percent of the time when investing in anything. If you are wrong about the investment value of a piece of linen, it won't be a total loss if you like the piece and have a use for it in your home.

How to Sell Linens and Lace

There are three rules to follow when selling any kind of antiques or collectibles.

Find a Knowledgeable Buyer

The first rule is to find a knowledgeable buyer. As with any antique or collectible, it is important to find a buyer who is able to identify the item(s) for sale and knows the market well enough to attach a fair price to them. Very few dealers in general antiques know the linens and lace markets. Knowledgeable buyers are usually dealers and collectors who specialize in the type of textiles you have.

In general, it is most profitable to sell to a collector. Since they plan to keep the item(s), they are usually willing to pay more than a dealer. However, there are a couple of weaknesses in this theory. As discussed earlier, remember that whether you are buying or selling, location is often a major factor in determining price. In addition, a collector is looking for items that he or she doesn't already have and may not be interested in buying your entire collection, even if everything you have is of good quality. A dealer, on the other hand, is more likely to buy in bulk.

If you have an exceptional collection and you are in an area where household linens bring low prices, it is best to contact a dealer from outside the area. If possible, it is a good idea to send the potential buyer photographs of a few of the best pieces in the collection and an inventory list.

When selling to dealers please appreciate their position. They need to make a profit on what they buy from you, and they need to pay the expenses they incur to sell your merchandise. Dealers cannot usually afford to pay a seller more than half of the retail price of an item. On the other hand, we have seen dealers buy an item to make as little as twenty percent. The profit a dealer seeks to make varies as per the individual dealer.

Obtain More Than One Offer

The second rule is to offer the piece(s) you have for sale to more than one person. Reputable dealers and collectors are willing to hold their offers for a few days and in many cases for as long as thirty days.

Keep the Collection Together

The third rule is to keep a collection together and sell it as a lot. Very often dealers and collectors want to buy only the best pieces from a collection. The best pieces are always easiest to sell, and once they are sold, you may have a difficult time selling the others. Please note that a discount is usually given if someone buys a whole collection. In other words, if your pieces sold individually would fetch $2,000.00, you should be prepared to sell the whole collection to one buyer for less than $2,000.00. The rationale for this is that you have saved time and energy by selling everything to one buyer. In essence, you have passed the burden of disposing of the less desirable pieces to the buyer.

Care and Maintenance

Most of the care and maintenance instructions in this chapter are meant for items of historic significance or investment potential where preservation is of primary importance. When we say historic importance, we mean items that are either of interest to museums or of great significance within your family such as items made by one of your ancestors that have been handed down from generation to generation. In particular, the instructions on how to clean linens and lace should be used with common sense. Obviously, not every piece merits the time and expense involved in museum quality cleaning.

Ease of care is clearly of major concern to most people when purchasing household linens for everyday use, and the vast majority of 20th century household linens and lace fall into this category. If you are prepared for the worst to happen, sturdy linens can be thrown in the washing machine on the gentle cycle using lukewarm water. If the piece has some lace trim, you may still be able to use the washing machine by putting the piece into a nylon mesh bag before putting it in the machine. Pieces with net and/or large amounts of lace should probably be hand washed. If there is any doubt in your mind, you are probably better off hand washing the item. Laundry detergents readily available in local supermarkets are usually sufficient to remove most stains. If the piece is heavily stained, you may want to try soaking the piece overnight with any of the stain removers available in local supermarkets. You might also wish to try using warm or hot water when putting these pieces in the washing machine.

Care and maintenance of valuable pieces in your collection is both an art and a science. It is ongoing and necessary to prolong the life of your linens and lace. In order to ensure maximum preservation of your important pieces, you must take light, humidity, temperature fluctuations, and air and water impurities into account. As mentioned earlier in this book, textiles are fragile and should be handled accordingly. You should not feel intimidated by the information contained in the rest of this chapter. Other than museum curators, very few people have the time, money, space, and storage facilities to follow every single piece of advice outlined below. If you do even one of the things discussed here, you will have taken a positive step towards preserving your important pieces. The following are some basic do's and don't's:

Display and Storage of Household Linens

Do not store your linens and lace in cedar (or any other type of wood) chests without protective coverings. The acid in the wood will, when in direct contact with any kind of textiles over a period of time, first create a brownish stain that is impossible to remove, then weaken the cloth, and eventually eat a hole through the textiles at the point of contact. The acid always leaves a brownish stain on fabric so whenever you see brown stains on a piece of linen or lace check to see if the fabric has been weakened at that spot.

Please note that wood products such as cardboard boxes and regular paper also have acid that can cause fiber deterioration as well. Therefore, you may want to go to the added expense of buying acid-free tissue paper and boxes to store your more valuable pieces. The typical stationery store does not carry acid-free material so you will have to go to an archival supply store.

The following are sources for acid-free storage boxes and tissue:

University Products, Inc.
P.O. Box 101
Holyoke, MA 01041-0101
(800) 628-1912

Light Impressions
Rochester, NY
(800) 828-9859

Woolfitt's Art Enterprises, Inc.
390 Dupont Street
Toronto, Ontario M5S 2R5

(416) 922-0933

Carr McLean Co.
461 Horner Avenue
Toronto, Ontario
(416) 252-3371

When storing your linens and lace, it is better to lay them flat or roll them. Textiles may be rolled on acid-free cardboard rolls or wooden poles. If cardboard rolls which are not acid-free are used, they should be wrapped in Mylar before the textile is rolled up. If raw wooden poles are used, they should be covered with at least two coats of oil-based paint or polyeurethane then wrapped in cotton batting which is held in place on the pole by a covering of unbleached cotton. This prevents the acid in the wood from coming in contact with the piece to be stored. Do not fold your linens and lace unless absolutely necessary. It is also a good idea not to fold your textiles along the same lines all the time. Pieces that have been folded for a long period of time eventually develop stress tears along the folds. We realize that larger pieces like bed coverings and banquet size tablecloths are usually folded due to space considerations. This is not a problem for items that are taken out and used regularly. However, if you have pieces that you want to fold and store for a long time, please use acid-free tissue paper or a clean piece of cloth between the folds. Do not use colored tissue paper. The dyes from the tissue may stain your linen. The tissue paper should be crumpled before being placed between the folds to avoid flattening the fibers along the folds.

Textiles need to breathe or they will start to rot. With this in mind, there are several things that you should avoid doing:

1) **Do not wrap your textiles in plastic** for long periods of time. The static in plastic acts as a magnet for dust so if the plastic container is left open or unsealed, it will pull the dust from the air right into your textiles. While sealed plastic containers do keep textiles safe from dust and grime, they also prevent the necessary air from circulating through the fibers. In addition, if the piece is even slightly damp when you put it in the plastic bag, mold will soon start to form. When in contact with moisture for long periods of time, some plastics produce hydrochloric acid which will eventually create holes in your textiles.

2) Take the pieces out of storage every few months to check on condition. Remember that even when a piece is stored it is still subject to pollution in the air which can eventually have an adverse effect on it. In addition, chemicals used in the cleaning process that are not completely removed by the final rinsing or chemicals transferred from you while you were handling the piece, such as hand lotion residue, can cause fibers to weaken and break over time. Mildew and mold could also develop if the piece was stored when it was

still slightly damp. Regularly checking your pieces will enable you to identify these problems early.

3) If you wish to frame a piece, make sure that there is some space between the glass and the linen and that the matt is acid-free. It can be stitched to the backing but not taped, stapled, or glued to hold it in place. After framing do not seal the back of the frame with paper. Air needs to circulate through the textile being framed. Tack a piece of fabric to the back of the frame to create a dust cover. This will allow the air to circulate while protecting the piece from dust. Be sure to replace or wash the dust cover when it becomes dirty.

Extreme changes in temperature are harmful for all textiles. Temperatures between sixty-five and seventy-five degrees Farenheit are recommended. For this reason, hanging textiles on exterior walls is not a good idea. In medieval times, tapestries were hung on the walls of castles partly as a decorative feature but, more importantly, as a means of blocking the damp and cold that constantly oozed from the rubble filled walls even in the height of summer. The constant exposure to the cold weakened the fibers causing the tapestries to become brittle over time. Even though modern houses have better insulation in exterior walls, these walls still experience changes in temperature that exceed the recommended range. For this same reason unheated attics and basements are also undesirable storage places. The kitchen is another place where valuable linen should not be displayed or stored. The swings in temperature in kitchens during the times when someone is cooking are undesirable. And finally, avoid placing your linens too close to heating units.

Too little or too much humidity can also damage textiles. Humidity levels between forty-five and fifty-five percent are recommended. Too little moisture dries out the fabric and makes the fibers too brittle while too much humidity can cause mold and mildew. Avoid storing your linens in bathroom closets where humidity levels can often rise above acceptable levels. For this same reason, laundry rooms should also be avoided. During the winter, when it gets very dry, it would be helpful to use a humidifier to maintain humidity at acceptable levels.

Frequent or constant exposure to ultraviolet light, such as sunshine or fluorescent lights, will eventually cause textiles to disintegrate. This is why so many old linen and lace curtains are in such poor condition. If you are thinking of framing some of your pieces, you can ask your framer about using glass that blocks out ultraviolet rays. However, you should note that it is also more expensive and slightly duller than regular glass. UV filters to cover your fluorescent lights can also be bought at your local electrical supply store. Exterior windows can be coated with a substance that blocks out ultraviolet rays - a practice followed by many museums. However, this can also be very expensive. Please note that these substances do not last forever and will need to be renewed periodically.

A less expensive way to protect your pieces would be to simply rotate them so that no one piece is exposed to ultraviolet rays for long periods of time. Items not in use should be stored in a dark place.

Linens and lace should be cleaned but not ironed before storing. Ironing makes fibers tense and brittle, thus increasing the risk of tears if the piece is stored in a folded position.

Do not put your new purchases in with the rest of your linens until you have thoroughly checked them for pests. If something has moth holes, do not assume that those are old moth holes. The item should be cleaned before being put away.

If you plan on leaving your linens on hangers or curtain rods for any length of time, you should pad the hangers and rods with cotton batting and then stitch unbleached cotton over the padding. The necessary materials are available at craft and quilting supply stores. Please note that gravity exerts pressure on the portion of fabric that is draped over the hanger or the curtain rod. Old clothing often shows wear around the shoulders for precisely this reason. Consequently, we do not recommend storing your linens on hangers. If you are using hangers or rods for display, we suggest rotating the pieces on display so that no one piece is subjected to constant pressure.

Some dealers refinish antique furniture with a type of wax which gives a look similar to a recently polished wood floor. If exposed to sunlight or some other source of high heat for some time, this wax can soften and stain fabric it comes into contact with. This wax is almost impossible to remove once it has rubbed off on your textiles. You should therefore exercise care when displaying linens on old quilt stands that have been refinished with wax.

Another way to display large pieces is to hang them from walls by using a hook and loop tape such as Velcro. The Velcro strips are stitched to fibreglass tape which, in turn, is tacked to the wall and stitched to the back of the piece you wish to hang. This is less harmful to the textiles than wood or metal curtain rods, hangers or quilt stands. Please note that the hook portion of the tape should go on the wall while the loop portion should be attached to the textile you wish to hang.

Cleaning of Household Linens

It is safer not to soak fragile antique lace in water or any other liquid because the lace is subject to stretching and tearing when wet. It is less traumatic for the piece if you lay a fiberglass window screen over it and gently vacuum the piece to remove dust and dirt. Do not put the vacuum too close to the fabric and be sure to use low suction. In addition, you may elect to put a screen over the vacuum nozzle also. If a piece is stained, you have to determine whether or not it is something you can live with. Any time you wash linens and lace you run the risk of damaging them.

For a number of reasons, museum curators prefer to keep pieces in their original condition as much as possible. They are interested in conserving pieces as opposed to restoring them to a useable condition. The rule of thumb in conservation is that whatever work is done on a piece should be reversible. Cleaning, unfortunately is not reversible. One example that is often used to demonstrate why it is so important to keep historically important pieces in their original condition goes as follows:

Your grandmother gives you a box of linen from her attic. One of the pieces is a man's linen shirt, initials A.L., with stains that appear to be blood. You wash the shirt and manage to get all the stains out. Afterwards, you indulge your curiosity about the contents of the box by trying to track down how it got into your grandmother's attic. You eventually trace the shirt's ownership back to a couple that worked for Abraham Lincoln when he was President. You then discover that the clothes Mr. Lincoln was wearing the night he was shot were probably part of a bundle of old clothing Mrs. Lincoln gave to this couple after the President's death. You now suspect that the shirt you found in your grandmother's box may be the shirt President Lincoln wore the night he died. This shirt is possibly an important piece of history but you now have no way to prove this because you destroyed the proof by washing all the stains out before you started your research. This is a classic case of an irreversible action. Obviously, this is an extreme case but it can happen. You can avoid major mistakes such as this by keeping the following in mind--when in doubt, don't!

We realize that most of the pieces you acquire will probably not be of major historical importance. However, it is one more thing to think about when you decide what you are going to do to your new acquisitions. Obviously, not cleaning anything may not be practical for the collector who wishes to use his or her pieces and not just display them.

It is less risky to soak small or medium-sized, sturdier pieces of lace. However, regardless of the condition of the piece, you should use lukewarm water when washing. In earlier times, linen was thrown in a big pot of boiling water to remove stains. This old-fashioned method is still followed by many people today. Unfortunately, textile conservators believe that hot or boiling water shocks the fibers which is detrimental to your pieces in the long run. In addition, hot water may shrink your lace and newer linens.

If the piece you intend to wash has some damage, you should repair the damaged area prior to washing it. After being soaked, the damaged ends will spread, change shape, and become much more difficult to repair.

Be careful about picking up the linen, particularly large pieces, when they are heavy with water because the weight of the water may cause the fabric to stretch and/or tear. Gently squeeze or press the excess water out of the linen when you are finished soaking. Do not wring the water out of your linens. If you do, you may twist them out of shape or tear the fibers. After discarding the excess water, you should air dry the linens. Do not use a clothes dryer; as discussed earlier, high heat is not desirable and may shrink your linens and lace.

We are even more reluctant to soak large lace pieces as well as pieces with lace insertions because we find them hard to handle when soaking wet. The chances of accidentally tearing the lace are much greater when trying to untangle wet lace. For this reason, we prefer to lay a piece out on a flat surface and gently sponge it down. It is much easier to pay special attention to the stained areas when the whole piece is laid out, as opposed to rolled up in a ball in a small tub of water. Do not rub the stained area. After sponging the piece, you can leave it to air dry. Do not hang the piece up when drying it because the weight of the water may cause the lace to stretch or even tear. If you must soak a large piece, place fiberglass window screens around it to form a "sandwich" before you begin. The screens will enable you to safely lift the wet lace from the tub or sink. When using this method, be sure to bind the screens' edges. This is done to protect the fabric.

Distilled water is best when washing antique and collectible linens and lace. Minerals in regular water can cause rust stains, which are very difficult to remove. However, this can get very expensive. A more economical way would be to use the distilled water only for the last rinse.

If plain water does not remove the stain, you can try a very mild, non-detergent soap called W.A. Paste. It was actually invented for veterinary use but has since been touted as a cleanser for antique textiles and is used by many museums today. You could also try wetting the area in question and sprinkling some baking powder on it. The baking powder should absorb the stain. After the area has dried, gently brush off the loose baking powder.

As discussed earlier, whatever cleaning agent agent you must use must be completely rinsed out of your textiles to avoid potential long-term damage. In addition, the fluorescent in detergents available today can cause white linen to look yellow under halogen lighting if any residue of the detergents remains in your textiles after the cleaning process.

It is difficult to list all the types of stain removers you can use on various kinds of stains. There are some good books on the market that discuss stain removal. There are also professional cleaners and textile conservators who specialize in cleaning expensive textiles. Your local museum's textile department will probably be able to recommend a textile conservator. You might also try calling your local theatre, opera, or ballet company to find out who they use to clean their costumes.

Many people, including dealers, love to starch and press their linens and lace. We have observed that crisply starched and pressed linens often sell faster and at higher prices than comparable unstarched pieces. Unfortunately, starching linens can be harmful to them. Starch attracts various pests and will absorb moisture which may cause mold and mildew. It is safer not to starch your linens before storing them. If you have purchased a heavily starched piece, you should remove the starch before storing it.

Repair of Linens and Lace

For particularly valuable pieces, it would be advisable to consult an expert. There are places that specialize in reweaving holes in linen and other fabrics. If you have a fragile or damaged piece, it is best to stablilize it before doing anything else to it. This is done by basting the entire piece, if it is small, to unbleached cotton. If the piece is large, baste the damaged areas only. Do not tape torn areas together. The tape may be difficult to remove without causing further damage to these areas.

Cataloging Your Collection

We advise collectors to keep records of all items in their collections. The records should include a description of each item, the provenance (if any), the date of acquisition, who the seller was, the purchase price, current value, the condition and any repair work that you have done to it. With reference to provenance, you should try to find out as much about the history of ownership of the piece as possible. Obviously, a piece previously owned by Marie Antoinette would be more valuable than a comparable piece with no established history. Keeping the original purchase receipt is also important especially if you purchased the piece from a very famous person, a well-known dealer, or a prestigious auction house.

Inventory records help collectors track the monetary appreciation of their collection. In addition, they are extremely useful in the event of a collector's death. In the latter case, they provide the family with information which can be used to determine the value of a collection during the dispersal of the estate.

Use of Linens and Lace

We think that it is important that people enjoy their collections. The majority of 20th century textiles are still able to withstand modern day use. People often tell us that they don't use their table linens because they fear getting stains on them. Stains will occur from time to time but they are easy to remove if you rinse the piece immediately. Do not let the stain set.

We do not agree on whether rare household linen should be used. Liz does not use any of her rare pieces. She keeps them in storage and takes them out only for occassional condition checks and when they are going to be photographed or shown. Peggy agrees that some of the more fragile, older pieces may not stand up to regular use; however, she uses even her finest pieces throughout her home.

There are many uses for old linens and lace. We cannot begin to list all of them in this section. We recommend that you be creative, especially with pieces that are distressed and crying for a second life. The following are just a few suggestions to spur your creativity:

Small, fragile pieces of linen and lace can be framed. Larger pieces can be backed by a strong fabric and then hung.

Lace often outlasts the fabric to which it is attached. When this happens, it can be reattached to something else. Damaged lace can be cut up to trim pillows, cushions, bed sheets, hand towels, etc. We even know of a dealer who specializes in using old lace to make lamp shades.

Worn tablecloths and bed sheets can be cut up and reassembled into pillowcases, smaller tablecloths, napkins and hand towels. Embroidered pieces with small holes in the fabric can be salvaged by embroidering over the holes and incorporating them into the existing overall pattern of embroidery.

Embroidered or lacy top sheets make great curtains. One of Peggy's clients has used a cutwork tablecloth as a shower curtain, while another turned two pairs of curtains into a dust ruffle for her child's bed.

Doilies and placemats can be used to make cushion covers. They are also useful as insertions in larger pieces such as tablecloths, curtains, and quilts. Bits and pieces of linen and lace can be used in quilts or lace samplers. They also make wonderful trim for pillows and other household items.

Recently, it has become fashionable to mix and match different sets of china and silver flatware to create very interesting table settings. This practice can be extended to placemats, napkins, and other table linens as well.

Whatever you decide to do with your old linens and lace, remember that they were made to be used and enjoyed. Recycling them into pieces that you can use is an excellent way of keeping the lace tradition alive.

Bibliography

Butterick Publishing Company. *Battenberg and Other Tape Laces, Techniques, Stitches and Designs*. New York: Dover Publications, Inc., 1988.

Caulfield, S.F.A. and Seward, Blanche C. *Encyclopedia of Needlework*. Republication (6 vols. in 2) of the Dictionary of Needlework, 2nd ed. London, 1887. New York: Dover Publications, Inc. 1972.

Cheetham, Linda. *The Innocent Researcher and the Museum*. The Museum Ethnographer's Group, University of Hull, Hull, England, 1987.

Cave, Oneone. *Cutwork Embroidery and How to Do It*. Revised republication of Linen Cutwork. London, 1963. New York: Dover Publications, Inc., 1982.

de Bonneville, Francoise. *The Book of Fine Linen*. Paris: Flammarion, 1994.

Earnshaw, Pat. *The Identification of Lace*. Aylesbury, Bucks, England: Shire Publications, 1980.

Earnshaw, Pat. *Bobbin and Needle Laces*. London, Batsford Limited, 1983.

Earnshaw, Pat. *Lace Machines and Machine Laces*, London, Batsford Limited, 1986.

Fuhrmann, Brigita. *Bobbin Lace: An Illustrated Guide to Traditional and Contemporary Techniques*. Republication of Bobbin Lace: A Contemporary Approach. 1976. New York: Dover Publications, Inc., 1985.

Gostelow, Mary. *Embroidery*. New York: Arco Publishing, Inc., 1983.

-----. *A World of Embroidery*. New York, Charles Scribner's Sons, 1975.

Harris, Jennifer. *Textiles, 5,000 Years*. New York: Harry N. Abrams, 1993.

Iklé, Ernest. *La Broderie Mecanique, 1828-1930*. Paris, 1931.

Jackson, Emily. *Old Handmade Lace, With a Dictionary of a Lace*. London, 1900. Republication. New York: Dover Publications, Inc., 1987.

Knight, Pauline. *Filet Lace Patterns*. London: B.T. Batsford Limited, 1990.

Kraatz, A. *Lace: History and Fashion*. London, 1989.

Levey, S. M. *Lace, A History*. Victoria and Albert Museum/ Mancy & Son, 1983.

Palliser, Mrs. Bury. *History of Lace*. Republication of the 4th ed., 1911. New York: Dover Publications, Inc., 1984.

Pfannschmidt, Ernst Erik. *Twentieth Century Lace*. New York: Charles Scribners' Sons, 1975.

Reigate, Emily. *An Illustrated Guide to Lace*. Woodbridge, Sussex, England: the Antique Collectors' Club Ltd., 1986.

Simeon, Margaret. *The History of Lace*. London: Stainer and Bell, 1979.

Schwab, Davide. *The Story of Lace and Embroidery*. New York: Fairchild Publications Inc., 1951.

Sommer, Elyse. *Textile Collector's Guide*. New York: Sovereign Books, 1978.

Toomer, Heather. *Lace, A Guide to Identification of Old Lace Types and Techniques*. London: B.T. Batsford Limited, 1989.

Warnick Kathleen and Nilsson, Shirley. *Legacy of Lace, Identifying, Collecting, and Preserving American Lace*. New York: Crown Publishers, Inc., 1988.

Price Guide

While no effort was spared while compiling the pricing information contained in this book, the authors cannot accept any liability for loss, financial or otherwise, which may be incurred by reliance placed on the information herein.

All the prices quoted in this book were derived by averaging prices of similar items in antique shops, thrift shops, specialty shops for antique and vintage linens and lace, antique shows, flea markets and auctions in the United States and Canada.

All the prices in this book are based on the assumption that the pieces are in excellent condition unless otherwise stated in the descriptions of the individual items.

Please note that prices have not been assigned to items from museum collections pictured in this book.

Chapter I - Appenzell and Appenzell Type Embroidery

Page	Photo No.	Description	US$ Price Range	
6	1/1	tablecloth	$2,000.00	$2,200.00
9	1/5	hand towel	$150.00	$165.00
10	1/6	pair pillowcases	$250.00	$300.00
12	1/8	round tablecloth	$375.00	$450.00
13	1/9	runner	$550.00	$600.00
14	1/10	pillowcase	$1,500.00	$1,800.00
16	1/12	handkerchief case	$300.00	$360.00
17	1/13	pair pillowcases with bed sheet	$350.00	$420.00
17	1/13	duvet cover with sham	$125.00	$150.00
18	1/14	tablecloth with 8 napkins	$1,100.00	$1,300.00
20	1/16	6 placemats	$600.00	$720.00
22	1/18	bed sheet	$350.00	$420.00
23	1/19	tray cover	$65.00	$75.00
24	1/20	round tablecloth	$750.00	$825.00
26	1/22	tea cloth	$350.00	$420.00

Chapter II - Battenberg and Other Tape Laces

Page	Photo No.	Description	US$ Price Range	
32	2/1	pair curtains	$500.00	$600.00
34	2/2	pair bed covers	$800.00	$850.00
36	2/4	round tea cloth	$100.00	$125.00
36	2/4	4 coasters	$16.00	$20.00
37	2/5	tablecloth with 12 napkins	$700.00	$800.00
39	2/7	runner	$65.00	$75.00

Chapter III - Bobbin Lace

Page	Photo No.	Description	US$ Price Range	
40	3/1	tablecloth	$75.00	$90.00
42	3/2	tea cloth	$175.00	$195.00
43	3/5	insertion piece	$45.00	$50.00
44	3/6	round tablecloth	$175.00	$185.00
45	3/8	tea cloth	$100.00	$135.00
46	3/10	round tablecloth	$450.00	$500.00
48	3/16	tablecloth	$1,500.00	$1,800.00
48	3/16	24 napkins	$250.00	$300.00
50	3/18	tray cover	$60.00	$65.00
50	3/18	doily	$30.00	$35.00
50	3/19	placemat	$75.00	$80.00
51	3/20	runner	$300.00	$360.00
52	3/21	12 placemats with napkins	$350.00	$420.00
53	3/22	pair curtains	$500.00	$600.00
54	3/23	sleigh bed cover	$350.00	$385.00
55	3/24	antimacassar set	$70.00	$80.00
56	3/25	12 napkins	$50.00	$60.00
56	3/26	12 napkins, placemats & a runner	$650.00	$715.00
57	3/27	runner	$35.00	$40.00
57	3/27	hand towel	$10.00	$12.00
57	3/27	4 napkins	$40.00	$44.00
57	3/27	5 Maltese doilies	$35.00	$40.00
57	3/27	coarse linen doilies	$3.00	$3.50
57	3/27	12 French doilies	$80.00	$88.00
57	3/27	6 linen x shaped doilies	$30.00	$36.00
57	3/27	10 bobbin lace doilies	$30.00	$36.00

Chapter IV - Chemical Lace and Other Machine Laces

Page	Photo No.	Description	US$ Price Range	
58	4/1	bed cover	$450.00	$500.00
60	4/2	pair curtains	$125.00	$150.00
61	4/3	sham	$75.00	$90.00
62	4/4	pillow	$65.00	$75.00
63	4/5	doily	$15.00	$18.00
63	4/6	tray cover	$60.00	$65.00
64	4/8	placemat	$35.00	$40.00
64	4/9	tablecloth	$45.00	$50.00
65	4/10	round tablecloth	$175.00	$195.00
66	4/11	runner	$100.00	$120.00
66	4/11	rectangular placemat	$20.00	$24.00
66	4/11	oval placemat	$7.00	$8.00
67	4/12	tablecloth	$50.00	$60.00
67	4/12	pair cushion covers	$100.00	$120.00
68	4/13	pair curtains	$125.00	$150.00
69	4/14	bed cover with 4 piece dresser set	$85.00	$100.00

Chapter V - Combinations of Lace

Page	Photo No.	Description	US$ Price Range	
72	5/2	tablecloth with 8 napkins	$125.00	$150.00
73	5/3	tea cloth	$150.00	$180.00
74	5/5	tea cloth	$65.00	$75.00
75	5/6	round tablecloth	$1,000.00	$1,200.00
76	5/9	runner	$75.00	$90.00
77	5/10	pillowcase	$25.00	$27.50
77	5/10	round doily	$27.50	$30.00
77	5/10	child's pillowcase	$40.00	$44.00
77	5/10	large square doily	$14.00	$15.00
77	5/10	small square doily	$9.00	$10.00
77	5/10	oval doily	$10.00	$11.00
77	5/10	hand towel	$25.00	$27.50
78	5/11	placemat	$40.00	$45.00
79	5/12	12 napkins	$120.00	$135.00
79	5/13	runner	$200.00	$220.00
79	5/13	12 napkins	$120.00	$135.00
80	5/14	lamp shade	$195.00	$230.00
81	5/15	pair bed covers	$900.00	$990.00
82	5/16	bed cover	$195.00	$225.00
83	5/17	bed cover	$275.00	$300.00
84	5/18	bed cover	$650.00	$700.00
86	5/22	bed cover	$425.00	$475.00
88	5/24	pair curtains	$500.00	$600.00
88	5/25	tea cloth	$90.00	$100.00
89	5/26	dresser scarf	$100.00	$110.00
89	5/26	cushion cover	$75.00	$90.00
90	5/27	tablecloth	$850.00	$950.00

Chapter VI - Crochet

Page	Photo No.	Description	US$ Price Range	
92	6/1	6 placemats	$30.00	$35.00
92	6/1	tea cozy	$20.00	$24.00
92	6/1	6 napkins	$30.00	$35.00
94	6/2	bread doily	$8.00	$8.80
94	6/2	coaster	$2.00	$2.40
94	6/2	hand towel	$10.00	$12.00
94	6/2	tray cover	$40.00	$45.00
94	6/3	tray cover	$12.00	$14.00
95	6/4	tray cover	$12.00	$14.00
95	6/5	tea cloth	$40.00	$44.00
96	6/6	runner	$75.00	$90.00
96	6/7	runner	$30.00	$33.00
96	6/7	napkin	$3.50	$4.00
96	6/8	antimacassar	$15.00	$18.00
97	6/9	antimacassar	$25.00	$30.00
97	6/9	cushion cover	$30.00	$35.00
97	6/9	bed cover	$150.00	$175.00
98	6/10	pair cushions	$70.00	$80.00
98	6/11	throw	$125.00	$150.00
99	6/12	curtain panel	$250.00	$275.00
100	6/13	pillowcase	$8.00	$9.00
100	6/14	placemat	$10.00	$12.00
102	6/16	curtain panel	$50.00	$60.00
102	6/17	doily	$5.00	$5.50
103	6/18	antimacassar set	$30.00	$33.00
103	6/18	figural pillow	$40.00	$44.00
103	6/18	bed cover	$175.00	$200.00
104	6/19	tablecloth	$150.00	$165.00
105	6/21	centerpiece	$5.00	$6.00
106	6/22	child's bed cover and sham	$275.00	$325.00
107	6/23	doily	$4.00	$4.50
107	6/24	doily	$8.00	$9.50
108	6/25	doily	$8.00	$9.50
109	6/26	trivet cover	$20.00	$22.00
109	6/26	12 coasters	$50.00	$60.00

Chapter VII - Cutwork

Page	Photo No.	Description	US$ Price Range	
110	7/1	tray cover	$35.00	$40.00
110	7/1	4 napkins	$20.00	$24.00
112	7/2	tea cloth	$65.00	$75.00
112	7/3	curtain panel	$100.00	$120.00

Page	Photo No.	Description	US$ Price Range	
113	7/4	curtain panel	$350.00	$385.00
114	7/5	bed sheet with pair pillowcases	$125.00	$150.00
115	7/6	framed cutwork cats	$100.00	$125.00
115	7/7	cushion cover	$75.00	$90.00
116	7/8	tablecloth with 12 napkins	$1000.00	$1200.00
118	7/10	tablecloth	$75.00	$90.00
119	7/11	runner	$30.00	$36.00
119	7/11	8 napkins	$40.00	$48.00
119	7/11	8 napkins	$40.00	$48.00
119	7/11	placemat	$12.00	$14.00

Chapter VIII - Embroidery

Page	Photo No.	Description	US$ Price Range	
120	8/1	tablecloth	$295.00	$350.00
122	8/2	8 placemats and napkins	$225.00	$245.00
123	8/3	round tablecloth	$100.00	$120.00
123	8/3	pillowcase	$15.00	$18.00
123	8/3	child's pillowcase	$40.00	$44.00
123	8/3	doily	$4.50	$5.00
123	8/3	coaster	$2.50	$3.00
124	8/4	bed sheet	$95.00	$110.00
125	8/5	bed sheet with pair pillowcases	$150.00	$180.00
126	8/6	bed sheet	$75.00	$90.00
126	8/6	sham	$40.00	$44.00
127	8/7	pair bed covers	$300.00	$330.00
128	8/8	8 placemats	$40.00	$44.00
128	8/8	5 placemats	$20.00	$24.00
128	8/8	runner	$25.00	$30.00
128	8/8	hand towel	$12.00	$13.00
129	8/9	placemat	$15.00	$18.00
129	8/9	6 napkins	$60.00	$70.00
130	8/10	tea cloth	$135.00	$150.00
131	8/11	tablecloth	$175.00	$210.00

Chapter IX - Fun Linen

Page	Photo No.	Description	US$ Price Range	
132	9/1	set of 7 towels	$35.00	$40.00
132	9/1	growth chart	$25.00	$30.00
132	9/1	laundry bag	$25.00	$30.00
132	9/1	3 napkins (each)	$2.00	$2.25
132	9/1	child's pillow	$15.00	$18.00
134	9/2	8 napkins	$30.00	$35.00
135	9/3	8 napkins	$30.00	$35.00
135	9/4	8 napkins	$40.00	$45.00
135	9/5	3 napkins and 10 coasters	$20.00	$24.00

Page	Photo No.	Description	US$ Price Range	
136	9/6	bed cover and 3 piece dresser set	$95.00	$110.00
137	9/7	cushion cover	$20.00	$24.00
137	9/7	tablecloth	$40.00	$45.00
137	9/8	framed cross–stitch piece	$20.00	$24.00

Chapter X - Linen Damask

Page	Photo No.	Description	US$ Price Range	
138	10/1	24 napkins	$250.00	$275.00
140	10/2	napkin	$10.00	$11.00
140	10/2	Art Deco towel	$14.00	$15.00
140	10/2	pink and white towell	$10.00	$11.00
140	10/2	Art Deco towel	$14.00	$15.00
140	10/2	Panama towel	$10.00	$11.00
141	10/3	tablecloth	$75.00	$90.00
142	10/4	tablecloth	$50.00	$60.00
143	10/5	yellow napkin	$4.00	$4.50
143	10/5	yellow and white napkin	$3.00	$3.50

Chapter XI - Needle Lace

Page	Photo No.	Description	US$ Price Range	
144	11/1	tea cloth	$400.00	$450.00
145	11/2	curtain panel	$700.00	$800.00
146	11/3	cushion cover	$90.00	$95.00
146	11/4	tablecloth	$175.00	$195.00
148	11/7	tablecloth	$10,000.00	$12,000.00
154	11/13	tablecloth	$2,250.00	$2,500.00
156	11/15	tablecloth border	$2,300.00	$2,500.00
160	11/19	placemat	$250.00	$300.00
161	11/20	placemat	$150.00	$175.00
162	11/21	antimacassar set	$50.00	$60.00
162	11/22	doily	$40.00	$45.00
163	11/23	4 placemats with napkins	$150.00	$165.00
163	11/23	Chinese placemat	$20.00	$22.00
163	11/23	5 coasters	$20.00	$24.00
164	11/24	pair bed covers	$3,600.00	$4,000.00
165	11/25	tablecloth	$300.00	$330.00

Chapter XII - Filet Lace and Buratto

Page	Photo No.	Description	US$ Price Range	
166	12/1	bed cover	$250.00	$275.00
168	12/2	runner	$50.00	$55.00
168	12/3	runner	$125.00	$150.00

Page	Photo No.	Description	US$ Price Range	
169	12/4	tablecloth	$200.00	$240.00
169	12/5	table cover	$150.00	$165.00
170	12/6	tablecloth	$150.00	$200.00
171	12/7	bed cover	$275.00	$300.00
171	12/7	portiere	$95.00	$105.00
172	12/8	filet lace panel	$80.00	$90.00
172	12/8	insertions (each)	$4.50	$5.50
172	12/8	butterflies (each)	$5.00	$5.50
173	12/9	pair curtains	$600.00	$660.00
174	12/11	runner	$35.00	$40.00
174	12/11	8 coasters	$24.00	$25.00
175	12/12	placemat	$30.00	$35.00
175	12/13	hand towel	$20.00	$25.00

Chapter XIII - Tatting

Page	Photo No.	Description	US$ Price Range	
176	13/1	bed sheet	$60.00	$65.00
178	13/2	pair pillowcases	$40.00	$45.00
179	13/3	beige doily	$5.00	$6.00
179	13/3	round doily	$5.00	$6.00
179	13/3	star shaped doily	$12.00	$14.00
179	13/3	pink and white doily	$8.00	$9.00
179	13/3	hand towel	$15.00	$16.50
179	13/3	placemat	$15.00	$18.00
179	13/3	runner	$30.00	$33.00
179	13/3	square mat	$15.00	$18.00

Chapter XIV - Types of Drawnwork

Page	Photo No.	Description	US$ Price Range	
180	14/1	tablecloth with 7 napkins	$400.00	$440.00
182	14/2	bed cover	$350.00	$420.00
183	14/3	bed sheet and sham	$175.00	$210.00
184	14/4	bed sheet	$75.00	$90.00
184	14/4	pair pillowcases	$60.00	$65.00
185	14/5	tablecloth	$500.00	$600.00
186	14/6	placemat	$20.00	$22.00
186	14/6	placemat	$20.00	$22.00
186	14/6	6 napkins	$30.00	$35.00
186	14/6	6 napkins	$30.00	$33.00
186	14/6	runner	$65.00	$78.00
187	14/7	runner	$70.00	$75.00
187	14/7	8 napkins	$40.00	$45.00
188	14/8	8 napkins	$90.00	$100.00
188	14/9	pair hand towels	$17.50	$20.00
189	14/10	tea cloth	$135.00	$150.00

Index

A

A World of Embroidery 121
acid-free cardboard rolls 199
acid-free material 199
acid-free matt 200
acid-free storage boxes 199
America/n (see United States, US, USA) 93, 177
antimacassar 96-97
antimacassar set 55, 102-103, 162
antique/s 5, 190, 192-193, 195-198,200-201
antique shops 193-194
antique show/s 93, 102, 105, 191,193-194, 196, 198
Appenzell 7-9, 28, 121, 196
Appenzell-type 6-7, 9-27, 29-31, 196
applique'/d 71, 122, 132-133, 135
Army/Navy tablecloth 70, 72, 193
Art Deco 139-141
Art Nouveau 12, 24-25
Asia 191
Atlanta 197
auction/s 6,144,193-194, 197
auction house/s 193-195, 202
Austria 121

B

Baltimore 197
Battenberg 32-39
Battenberg and Other Tape Laces 33
bed cover/s 33-34, 36, 39, 57-59, 69, 71, 81-87, 93, 97, 102-103, 106, 127, 136, 139, 164, 166-167, 171, 174, 177, 181-182, 190
bed sheet/s 10, 17, 22-23, 59, 94, 124-127, 167, 176-177, 183-184, 190, 193, 196-197, 202
bedspreads (see bed cover/s) 93
Belgium 33-34
bobbin lace/s 33, 35, 40-57, 60-61, 64, 71, 80, 82-84, 86-89, 128, 136, 171, 177, 191
bobbin lace applique' 71

bobbin lace insert/s/ions 42-44, 46-47, 54, 56-57, 71, 82-84, 86-89, 173
bone lace (bobbin lace) 41
braids(tapes) 33
bread doily 94
bread tray cover 94
brides 33, 35, 41, 59, 154-155, 181, 195
Broderie Anglaise (eyelet) 121
Brooklyn 192
Brooklyn Museum 192
Bruge (see Battenberg) 33
buratto 6, 9, 14-15, 167-168, 173, 175, 185
Burnand, Eugene 7
burned lace (Chemical lace) 59
Butterick Publishing Company 33
buttonhole stitch/s 111, 129, 145, 181

C

California 192
Canada/Canadian 5,33,81, 104, 197
Cantu 33, 41, 48-49, 51-52, 55-57, 191
Care and Maintenance 191, 198-199
Cataloging your Collection 202
Cheetham, Linda 192
Chemical lace 59, 63-66, 195
Chicago 192
child's pillowcase 77, 123, 132-133
China (see Chinese) 33, 41, 48, 57, 72, 109, 111, 145, 163, 165, 167, 174, 177, 181, 189, 196
Chinese (see China) 41, 48, 57, 72, 93, 109, 145, 154, 163, 167, 174, 191
clean/ing 198, 200-201
Cleaning of Household Linens 202
cloth (see tablecloth) 35, 42, 46, 67, 71-73, 146, 148, 165, 181, 185, 196, 199
Cluny (see Battenburg) 33
coaster/s 36, 94, 109, 123, 135, 163, 174
cocktail napkins 56, 132-135, 191
collectible/s/ility 5-6, 33, 39, 41, 46, 50, 56-57, 59, 62-63, 65-66, 71-72, 76-80, 84, 86, 88, 90, 93, 96, 98-99, 102, 104, 106, 112, 114-116, 118, 121, 123, 128-29, 131, 133,

141-142, 144-145, 156, 162, 164, 166-169, 173, 175, 183, 186, 190-193, 195-197, 198, 201
colored damask 139, 141
Combinations of Lace 70-91
condition 5, 53, 59, 63, 65, 71, 76, 79, 81, 86, 88, 100, 104, 115-116,156, 160-161, 169-171, 173, 181, 189,194-202
Cooper-Hewitt Museum 7, 192
couchwork 120-121
crochet/ed 92-109, 112, 190-191, 194, 197
crocheted insert/ion 94-95
cross-stitch 128, 132, 137
curtain/s(see curtain panel/s) 32-33, 36, 39, 53, 57, 60, 68, 88, 93, 96, 102, 112, 145, 167, 173-174, 191, 200, 202
curtain panel/s (see curtain/s) 53, 68, 93, 112, 145, 167
cushion/s 98, 167, 177, 202
cushion cover/s 28, 41, 67, 71, 81, 89, 97, 115, 136-137, 146, 167, 202
cutwork 46, 56, 70-71, 73, 75-80, 84-85, 90-91, 110-119,121, 125, 139, 144-145, 162, 181, 194, 196, 202
Cyprus 145

D

damask/s (see linen damask) 79, 94, 138-143, 178-179, 191, 197
de Bonneville, Francoise 139
Display and Storage of Household Linens 199-200
doily/ies 7-8, 33, 50, 57, 59, 63, 71, 77, 81, 93, 102, 107-109, 123, 162, 167, 177-179,197, 202
Don Quixote 29-31
double damask 139
drawn thread stitch (see drawnwork) 7
drawn threadwork(see drawnwork) 181
drawnwork 5, 6, 8-15, 17-31, 36, 39, 42-43, 45,50,54, 72, 86-87, 124, 126-128, 130, 142, 178, 180-191, 194
dresser scarf/ves 69, 89, 136

dresser set 69
Duchesse (see Battenburg) 33
duvet cover 7, 17

Earnshaw, Pat 192
East Coast 197
Education: Preparation for the Search 191-192
Egypt 121, 181
embroidery/ed 5-31, 37, 46, 70-77, 81, 83, 86-87, 90-91, 111-113, 120-137, 139, 145, 167,171,177, 181, 183, 187-191,196-197, 202
England 41, 83, 95, 167, 171,193, 197
Europe/an 5, 41, 72, 93, 121, 145, 167, 174, 177, 181, 191, 193, 195, 197
eyelet 74-75, 79, 121, 123-124, 129, 131

fagoting 71
Far East 5
filet brode (fillet lace) 167
filet crochet/ed 93-103, 106
filet lace 62-63, 68, 70-73, 75-80, 82, 84, 88, 90-91,93, 115, 166-175, 181, 190,196, 198
filet lace insert/s/ions 68, 70-72, 75-77, 79-80, 82, 84, 88, 90-91,167, 172-173, 190, 196
Filet Lace Patterns 167
flea markets 33, 93, 102, 105, 190, 193-196
Flemish (see Battenburg) 33, 50
France(see French) 7, 57, 67, 81, 89, 121, 139, 145
French (see France) 66
French silk 57
Fun Linen 121, 132-137

generic crochet 93
German/y 7, 17, 121
Gostelow, Mary 121
Greece 121
growth chart 132-133

Hand Run Alencon 67
hand towel/s 9, 57, 59, 77, 94, 128, 140-141, 167, 175, 178-179, 188, 202
handkerchief case 16
handkerchief linen 60
Harris, Jennifer 139
Hillwood Museum 192
historic importance 198, 201
Hong Kong 191

Honiton (see Battenburg) 33
house sales 93, 193-195
household linen/s 5, 7, 33, 41, 75, 77, 111-112, 121, 123, 145, 181, 189, 191-193, 195-200, 202
How to Sell Linens and Lace 198
Hungary 121

Ikle' Ernest 7
Illinois 192
Investment Potential 195, 197-198
Ireland 74, 93, 139, 141
Irish crochet/ed 74, 93, 102-103, 108-109
Irish crocheted insertion 74
Irish linen 197
ironing 200
Italian (see Italy) 5, 163, 190-191
Italy (see Italian) 5, 48-49, 51-52, 55-56, 70-71, 75, 78-80, 84-85, 110-111, 115, 121, 124, 126-127, 139, 144-164, 167-168, 175, 180-181, 183-185, 190

Japan 191
Japanese 191

kitchen towels 133
Knight, Pauline 167

La Broderie Mecanique 7
Lace, A Guide to Identification of Old Lace Types and Techniques 192
Lace Collector Newsletter 41
lace samplers (Normandy lace or patchwork lace) 71, 81, 202
lacis (fillet lace) 167
lamp shade/s 80, 202
laundry bag 132-133
Legacy of Lace 177, 192
Linen Damask (see damask) 79, 138-143
Libya 121
London 193

machine chain stitch, 60
machine embroidery/ed 58-59, 183
machine-made lace 50, 53, 58-69, 71, 76-77, 81, 89, 120-121, 136, 145, 191-193
machine-made net 32, 41, 53, 57, 59, 71, 88-89, 146, 167

Maderia 76, 110-111, 116-119, 121-122, 125, 134-135
Maderia Work(see Maderia) 121
maintenance 198-199
Majorca 7, 29-31
Maltese lace 57
Marie Antoinette(see Battenberg) 33
Market Conditions 190-191
migration 194
moire' 58
monogram/s/ed 9-10, 17, 22-23, 38, 124, 185, 195-196
Montreal 197
mosiac(see drawnwork) 181
multi-colored damask 139
multi-colored embroidery 72, 121, 128, 132-133, 136-137
Musee des Arts Decorotifs 14
museum/s 5, 148, 190, 192, 198-201
mylar 199

napkin/s 7, 18, 29-30, 37-38, 41, 48, 52, 56-57, 59, 71-72, 79, 92-93, 96, 110-111, 116, 118-119, 122, 129, 132-135, 138-141, 143, 163, 167, 180-181, 186-188, 191, 196-197, 202
needle lace/s 33, 48, 59, 71, 75-79, 86-88, 107, 144-165, 167, 171, 177, 190-191, 196
needle lace applique' 71
needle lace insert/s/ions 71, 75-79, 86-88, 144, 146-147, 190, 196
Negotiating Prices 196
net darning 167
New York (NY) 17, 139, 191-192, 197
Nilsson, Shirley 177, 192
Normandy lace(patchwork lace or lace samplers) 71, 81
North America/n 5, 41, 81, 93, 167, 174, 181, 195, 197
NY (New York) 192, 199

Ontario 192, 199
organdy 56, 121-122, 135
organdy insertion 122
Ottawa 197

padded satin stitch 7, 28
panel (see curtain panel/s and curtain/s) 53, 60, 88, 112-113, 173
patchwork lace(Normandy lace or lace samplers) 71, 81
Peoples' Republic of China 191

Persia 121
Pfannschmidt, Ernst Eric 191
Philadelphia 139, 190
Philadelphia College of Textiles and Science 35, 40-41, 70-71, 101, 105, 178
Philippines 191
pillow/s 40-41, 62, 102-103, 202
pillow lace (bobbin lace) 41
pillowcase/s (see child's pillowcase) 9-11, 14-15, 17, 20, 23, 59, 77, 94, 100, 114, 123, 125, 132, 167, 178, 184, 193-194, 196, 202
pineapple design 107
placemats/s 20-21, 41, 48, 50, 52, 56, 59, 64, 66, 78, 92-93, 100, 118-119, 122, 128-129, 139, 160-161, 163, 167, 174-175, 178-179, 186, 196-197, 202
point de venise 71, 154-155, 164, 191, 196
point lace (see Battenberg) 33
portiere 171
Portugal(see Maderia) 116-118, 122, 135
pricing 5, 53, 196
printed cotton tablecloth 136-137
Providence 192
pulled threadwork (see drawnwork) 181
punchwork (see drawnwork and punchwork mosiac) 181, 185-188
punchwork mosiac (see drawnwork and punchwork) 181, 183-185
punto in aria 145

Quaker Lace Company 59

Repair of Linens and Lace 202
Reticella (needle lace) 145
Rhode Island 192
Rhode Island School of Design 192
Rumania 121
runner/s 12-13, 36, 39, 41, 48, 51, 56-57, 59, 66, 71, 76, 79, 81, 96, 118-119, 128, 139, 163, 167-168, 175, 178-179, 186-187, 196
Russian (see Battenburg) 33

salting 194
satin stitch/es 6-7, 9-11, 14-16, 22-25, 28, 72, 75
Sellers Return Policy 196
shadow stitch 124

sham/s 7, 17, 60-61, 106, 126-127, 183, 194
sheet/s (see bed sheet) 22-23, 114, 183-184, 193, 202
silk damask 139
sleigh bed cover 54
South America 5
Spain 145
Spanish Balearie Islands 121
starch 201
storage 199
Sunnyvale 192
Swiss embroidery (eyelet embroidery) 121
Switzerland 7-8, 28-30, 121

table cover(see tablecloth) 169
tablecloth/s 6-7, 10, 12, 18-19, 24-25, 29-31, 33, 35, 37-38, 40-41, 44, 46, 48-49, 51, 59, 64-65, 67, 70-72, 74-76, 81, 90-91, 101, 104-105, 116-118, 120-121, 123, 131, 136, 139, 141-142, 144-146, 148-156, 163-165, 167, 169, 170, 174, 177, 180-181, 185, 190-191, 193-194, 196-198, 199, 202
tag sales 195
tape lace/s (see Battenberg) 32-39, 41, 55, 57, 89, 144
tatted/ing 176-179, 187, 197
tatted inserts/ions 177-179
tea cloth/s 20, 26-27, 33, 36, 42-43, 45, 59, 73-74, 88, 95, 112, 130, 144, 167, 189
tea cozy 92-93
Tenerife (see Tenerife Lace) 121
Tenerife lace 182
Textiles-Five Thousand Years 139
Textilmuseum mit Textilbibliothek 7-8, 28-31
The Art Institute of Chicago 192
The Art of Collecting 191
The Book of Fine Linen 139
The Identification of Lace 192
The Innocent Researcher and the Museum 192
The Lace Museum 192
The Metropolitan Museum of Art 192
The Museum for Textiles 192
The Paley Design Center 35, 40-41, 70-71, 101, 105, 178
The Peoples Republic of China 191
The Royal Ontario Museum 192
thrift shops 193, 195
Tools of the Trade 193
Toomer, Heather 191, 192
Toronto 33, 93, 144, 192, 197, 199

towel/s (see hand towel/s) 9, 12, 57, 77, 128, 132-133, 140-141, 175, 178, 188, 197, 202
tray cover 23, 50, 63, 94-95, 110-111
tray cloth (see tray cover) 167
trivet cover 109
trousseau/s 6, 22-23, 121, 126-127, 172-173
turn of the century 5, 34-36, 70-71, 80-83, 88, 93, 96, 99, 115, 120-121, 145, 156-159, 164, 168, 172-173, 178
Twentieth Century Lace 191

Ulrich, H.C. 7-8
United States (see also US, USA, and America) 5, 33, 93, 102, 104, 121, 190-193, 197
Upgrading your Collection 196
US (see United States, USA, and America) 17, 93, 197
US East Coast 93
US Midwest 93, 197
USA (see America, United States, and US) 60, 65, 82, 92-109, 120-121, 128, 130, 136-137, 176-179
Use of Linens and Lace 202
Useful Measurements to Know 196

vanity set 136
velcro 200
vellum 40-41, 145
Venetian 41, 55-57
Venice 48-49, 51-52, 55-56, 145, 162, 190
vetted/ing 193
Victorian/a 32, 55, 80, 121, 167-168, 193-194
vintage linens and lace(see vintage textiles) 190, 197
vintage textiles(see vintage linens and lace) 5, 17, 193
viole 121

W.A. Paste 2, 101
Washington, D.C. 192, 197
Washington Crossing the Delaware 59
Warnick, Kathleen 177, 192
Western Europe/an 191, 197
Where to Buy-Sources 193
white damask 139
whitework 6-31, 121